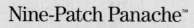

Nine-Patch Panache™

Editor **Carolyn S. Vagts**
Creative Director **Brad Snow**
Publishing Services Director **Brenda Gallmeyer**

Editorial Assistant **Carol Listenberger**
Graphic Designer **Nick Pierce**
Copy Supervisor **Deborah Morgan**
Copy Editors **Emily Carter, Mary O'Donnell**
Technical Editor **Angie Buckles**
Technical Proofreader **Sandra L. Hatch**
Technical Artist **Debera Kuntz**

Production Artist Supervisor **Erin Brandt**
Production Artists **Glenda Chamberlain,**
Edith Teegarden
Production Assistants **Marj Morgan,**
Judy Neuenschwander

Photography Supervisor **Tammy Christian**
Photography **Matthew Owen**
Photography Assistants **Tammy Liechty,**
Tammy Steiner

Nine-Patch Panache is published by Annie's, 306 East Parr Road, Berne, IN 46711. Printed in USA. Copyright © 2012 Annie's. All rights reserved. This publication may not be reproduced in part or in whole without written permission from the publisher.

Printed in the United States
Library of Congress Control Number: 2012937965
Softcover ISBN: 978-1-59217-377-8

RETAIL STORES: If you would like to carry this pattern book or any other Annie's publications, visit AnniesWSL.com

Every effort has been made to ensure that the instructions in this pattern book are complete and accurate. We cannot, however, take responsibility for human error, typographical mistakes or variations in individual work. Please visit ClotildeCustomerCare.com to check for pattern updates.

1 2 3 4 5 6 7 8 9 10

Welcome

Nine-Patch designs are amazing. There are so many combinations and ways to set a Nine-Patch block. Years could be spent compiling the patterns and all the different options. Instead of trying to bring you all of them, which would have been impossible, we are bringing you what we consider the best.

Here you will find all the patterns you will need to create quilt after quilt. Each pattern within these pages promises new and exciting options for creativity. Take the time to really look at the piecing. Sometimes, what you're looking for has been right there all the time. Take a second look at the Nine-Patch and discover a treasure trove of possibilities. You will probably be surprised to learn that many of your favorite blocks are Nine-Patch.

You can dress up these blocks or keep them simple. Your fabrics will give you all the options to change the entire feel. What's so fun about these blocks is that they never look the same twice if you experiment with the fabrics. Go ahead and explore! Your stash is the perfect place to start.

This book is a collection of some of the best Nine-Patch designs available. Our hope is that you take these Nine-Patch variations and create a quilt that will make you proud of your accomplishment, inspire you to explore more Nine-Patch possibilities and enjoy the process.

Carolyn S. Vagts

Contents

Classic Nines

- **4** Patriotic Star Log Cabin
- **8** Floating Stars
- **12** Nine-Patch Squared
- **15** Sashed Pinwheels Bed Runner
- **18** Reunion
- **21** Got the Blues
- **24** Cabin in the Woods
- **28** Square Dance

Romancing the Nines

- **32** Bloomin' Topper
- **35** Blizzard in Blue Bed Quilt
- **40** Toile Wreaths
- **43** Dewdrops
- **47** Romantic Heart
- **50** As the Geese Fly!
- **53** Nine-Patch Twirl
- **56** Beach Buddy
- **58** Weathervane Stars

Dressed to the Nines

- **63** Stars Squared
- **68** Royal Cherries
- **73** Dots & Prints
- **76** An Autumn Evening
- **80** Spring Fling
- **84** Dragonfly Rings
- **88** Swirling Pinwheels
- **91** Jitter Buzz
- **98** Cartwheels

Origins of Nines

- **102** Four-in-Nine-Patch Zigzag
- **105** The Harvester
- **111** Wolf Song
- **114** Mystic Chords of Memory
- **119** Stripes & Nine-Patches
- **122** This & That
- **126** Flying in Formation
- **129** Nine-Patch Appliqué Quilt & Bed Runner
- **134** Clowning Around

Sweet Nines

- **141** In the Meadow
- **144** Star Bright
- **148** Optica
- **151** Nine-Patch Heart Hot Mat
- **154** Basket Table Topper
- **158** Williamsburg Table Collection
- **162** In the Woods
- **166** Stars Around
- **169** Rose Blue

- **174** Project Gallery
- **176** Finishing Your Quilt
- **176** Special Thanks

Classic Nines

Here are classic Nine-Patch quilt designs to inspire you to create a masterpiece. With imagination and your own fabric choices, these classics can be anything you want them to be.

Patriotic Star Log Cabin

Join three very different blocks together to make this stunning patriotic quilt.

DESIGN BY PAT FORKE FROM QUAKERTOWN QUILTS

PROJECT SPECIFICATIONS

Skill Level: Intermediate
Quilt Size: 74" x 92"
Block Size: 9" x 9"
Number of Blocks: 63"

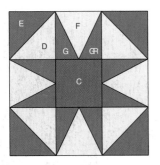

54-40 or Fight
9" x 9" Block
Make 18

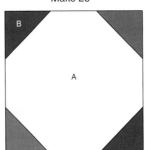

Log Cabin
9" x 9" Block
Make 28

Puss in the Corner
9" x 9" Block
Make 17

MATERIALS

- ⅓ yard each
  4 red/rust prints
- ⅝ yard each 5 cream prints
- ¾ yard rust star print
- 1 yard each 3 navy prints
- 1 yard cream tonal
- 1⅔ yards navy star print
- Backing 80" x 98"
- Batting 80" x 98"
- Neutral-color all-purpose thread
- Quilting thread
- Template material
- Basic sewing tools and supplies

Cutting

1. Cut (17) 9½" A squares from cream prints.

2. Cut five 1¾" by fabric width strips each cream print; subcut strips into 28 total of each of the following pieces: 1¾" x 2" I, 1¾" x 3¼" J, 1¾" x 4½" M, 1¾" x 5¾" N, 1¾" x 7" Q and 1¾" x 8¼" R. ***Note:*** *Cut I and J, M and N, and Q and R pieces in pairs from the fabrics.*

3. Cut eight 1¾" by fabric width strips each navy and navy star prints; subcut strips into 28 total of each of the following pieces: 1¾" x 3¼" K, 1¾" x 4½" L, 1¾" x 5¾" O, 1¾" x 7" P, 1¾" x 8¼" S and 1¾" x 9½" T. ***Note:*** *Cut K and L, O and P, and S and T pieces in pairs from the fabrics.*

4. Prepare templates for F and G using patterns given.

5. Cut five 3½" by fabric width strips total navy and navy star prints; using the G template, subcut strips into 18 sets of four each G and GR pieces as shown in Figure 1.

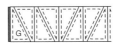

Figure 1

6. Cut one 3⅞" by fabric width strip each navy and navy star prints; subcut strips into 18 sets of two 3⅞" squares to match G/GR sets. Cut each square in half on one diagonal to make 18 sets of four E triangles.

7. Cut nine 4½" by fabric width strips total navy and navy star prints; subcut strips into the following: six 4½" x 10½" W rectangles, (12) 4½" x 8½" X rectangles, (16) 4½" x 6½" Y rectangles and (16) 4½" Z squares.

8. Cut four 3⅞" by fabric width strips cream tonal; subcut strips into (36) 3⅞" squares. Cut each square in half on one diagonal to make 72 D triangles.

9. Cut four 3½" by fabric width strips cream tonal; using the F template, subcut strips into 72 F pieces as shown in Figure 2.

Figure 2

10. Cut eight 3½" by fabric width strips total red/rust and rust star prints; subcut strips into (68) 3½" B squares and (18) 3½" C squares. Draw a diagonal line from corner to corner on the wrong side of each B square.

11. Cut 28 total 2" H squares rust/red and rust star prints.

12. Cut eight 2" by fabric width strips rust star print. Join strips on short ends to make one long strip; press seams open. Subcut strip into two 2" x 81½" U strips and two 2" x 66½" V strips.

13. Cut nine 2¼" by fabric width strips navy star print for binding.

Completing the Puss in the Corner Blocks

1. Place a B square right sides together on each corner of A and stitch on the marked lines as shown in Figure 3.

Figure 3

2. Trim seam to ¼" and press B to the right side to complete one Puss in the Corner block.

3. Repeat steps 1 and 2 to make 17 Puss in the Corner blocks.

Completing the 54-40 or Fight Blocks

1. To complete one 54-40 or Fight block, select four each E, G and GR same-fabric pieces, and four each D and F pieces. Sew G and GR to F as shown in Figure 4; press seams away from F. Repeat to make four F-G units.

Figure 4

2. Sew D to E along the diagonal to make a D-E unit as shown in Figure 5; press seam toward E. Repeat to make four D-E units.

Figure 5

3. Sew an F-G unit to opposite sides of C to make the center row as shown in Figure 6; press seams toward C.

4. Sew a D-E unit to opposite sides of an F-G unit to make the top row, again referring to Figure 6; press seams toward the D-E units. Repeat to make the bottom row.

Figure 6

5. Sew the center row between the top and bottom rows referring to the block drawing to complete one 54-40 or Fight block; press seams toward the center row. Repeat to make 18 blocks.

6. Repeat steps 1–5 to make (18) 54-40 or Fight blocks.

Completing the Log Cabin Blocks

1. To complete one Log Cabin block, sew I to one side of H; press seam toward I.

2. Sew J to the H-I unit as shown in Figure 7; press seam toward J.

Figure 7

3. Continue to add strips around the center in alphabetical order referring to the block drawing to complete one Log Cabin block; press seams toward the most recently added strips as you stitch.

4. Repeat steps 1–3 to make 28 Log Cabin blocks.

Completing the Quilt

1. Join two Puss in the Corner blocks with three 54-40 or Fight blocks to make an XX row as shown in Figure 8; press seams toward the Puss in the Corner blocks. Repeat to make four XX rows.

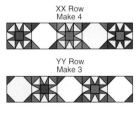

Figure 8

2. Join two 54-40 or Fight blocks with three Puss in the Corner blocks to make a YY row, again referring to Figure 8; press seams toward the Puss in the Corner blocks. Repeat to make three YY rows.

3. Join the XX and YY rows to complete the pieced center referring to the Placement Diagram for positioning; press seams in one direction.

4. Join seven Log Cabin blocks to make a side row as shown in Figure 9; press seams in the opposite direction from the pieced top. Repeat to make two side rows.

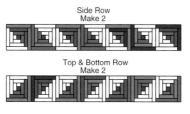

Side Row
Make 2

Top & Bottom Row
Make 2

Figure 9

5. Sew a side row to opposite long sides of the pieced center referring to the Placement Diagram for positioning; press seams toward the side rows.

6. Join seven Log Cabin blocks to make the top row, again referring to Figure 9; press seams in opposite directions from the pieced center. Repeat to make the bottom row.

7. Sew the top and bottom rows to the pieced center referring to the Placement Diagram for positioning; press seams toward top and bottom rows.

8. Sew U strips to opposite long sides and V strips to the top and bottom of the pieced center; press seams toward the U and V strips.

9. Join the W, X, Y and Z pieces to make two side borders and a top and bottom border referring to the Placement Diagram; press seams in one direction.

10. Sew the pieced side borders to the opposite long sides first and add the pieced top and bottom borders to complete the top; press seams toward the U and V strips.

11. Layer, quilt and bind referring to Finishing Your Quilt on page 176. ■

Patriotic Star Log Cabin
Placement Diagram 74" x 92"

F
Cut 72 cream tonal

G
Cut 144 total navy
& navy star prints
(reverse half for GR)

Floating Stars

Two fabrics with good contrast and a classic Nine-Patch block make this quilt a rare beauty.

DESIGNED AND QUILTED BY TRICIA LYNN MALONEY

PROJECT SPECIFICATIONS

Skill Level: Confident Beginner
Quilt Size: 58" x 71½"
Block Size: 12" x 12"
Number of Blocks: 12

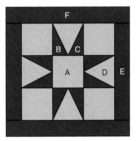

Framed Floating Star
12" x 12" Block
Make 12

MATERIALS

- 2½ yards coordinating dark tonal
- 3 yards floral print
- Batting 66" x 80"
- Backing 66" x 80"
- Neutral-color all-purpose thread
- Quilting thread
- Basic sewing tools and supplies

Cutting

1. Cut six 2¼" by fabric width dark tonal strips; subcut strips into (48) 2¼" x 4⅞" B/C rectangles.

2. Cut (14) 2" by fabric width dark tonal strips; subcut strips into (24) 2" x 9½" E strips and (24) 2" x 12½" F strips.

3. Cut six 3½" by fabric width dark tonal J/K strips.

4. Cut seven 2¼" by fabric width dark tonal strips for binding.

5. Cut five 3½" by fabric width floral print strips; subcut strips into (60) 3½" A squares.

6. Cut five 3⅞" by fabric width floral print strips; subcut strips into (48) 3⅞" D squares.

7. Cut eight 2" by fabric width floral print strips; subcut strips into eight 2" x 12½" G sashing strips and five 2" x 39½" H sashing strips.

8. Cut three 2" by fabric width floral print I strips.

9. Cut seven 5½" by fabric width floral print L/M strips.

Completing the Blocks

1. Mark the center of one side edge of each D square.

2. Position a straightedge from the center mark to the lower right-hand corner of D and trim with a rotary cutter as shown in Figure 1.

Figure 1

3. Repeat on the opposite side of D as shown in Figure 2 to make a triangle. Discard trimmed triangles. Repeat to make 48 D triangles.

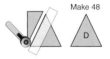

Figure 2

4. Position a straightedge from left bottom corner to top right corner of a B/C rectangle as shown in Figure 3 and cut with rotary cutter. Repeat with a total of 24 B/C rectangles to make 48 B star points.

Figure 3

5. Position a straightedge from top left corner to right bottom corner of a B/C rectangle as shown in Figure 4 and cut with rotary cutter. Repeat with remaining B/C rectangles to make 48 C star points.

Figure 4

6. Stitch C to the left side of D as shown in Figure 5; press seam toward C.

Figure 5

7. Stitch B to right side of D as shown in Figure 6; press seam toward D.

Figure 6

8. Repeat steps 6 and 7 to make 48 star point units, again referring to Figure 6.

9. To complete one block, stitch one star point unit between two A squares to make a top row referring to Figure 7; press seams in one direction. Repeat to make a bottom row.

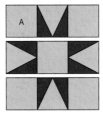

Figure 7

10. Stitch an A square between two star point units, again referring to Figure 7, to make a center row; press seams in opposite direction of top/bottom rows.

11. Stitch rows together, matching seams to make the Nine-Patch block center, again referring to Figure 7.

12. Stitch two E strips to opposite sides and then two F strips to the top and bottom of Nine-Patch block center referring to the block drawing. Press seams toward E and F.

13. Repeat steps 9–12 to make 12 Framed Floating Star blocks.

Completing the Quilt

1. Stitch two G sashing strips and three blocks together to make a row as shown in Figure 8; press seams toward G. Repeat to make four rows.

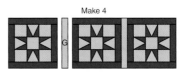

Figure 8

2. Stitch rows together with five H sashing strips, beginning and ending with H as shown in Figure 9. Press seams toward H.

Figure 9

3. Join the I strips together on short ends to make one long strip; press seams open. Subcut strip into two 2" x 56" I sashing strips. Referring to the Placement Diagram, sew I strips to opposite sides of the pieced sashing and blocks unit to complete the pieced center; press seams toward I.

4. Join the J/K strips together on short ends to make one long strip; press seams open. Subcut strip into two 3½" x 42½" J borders and two 3½" x 62" K borders.

5. Sew J to top and bottom of pieced center and K to opposite long sides, again referring to the Placement Diagram. Press seams toward J and K.

6. Join the L/M strips together on short ends to make one long strip; press seams open. Subcut strip into two 5½" x 48½" L borders and two 5½" x 72" M borders.

7. Sew L to top and bottom of pieced center and M to opposite long sides, again referring to the Placement Diagram. Press seams toward L and M.

8. Layer, quilt and bind referring to Finishing Your Quilt on page 176. ◼

Floating Stars
Placement Diagram 58" x 71½"

Nine-Patch Squared

Tiny squares were used in the Nine-Patch block centers of this well-worn, turn-of-the-century quilt. Use rotary-cutting methods to recreate its timeless beauty.

DESIGN BY SANDRA L. HATCH

PROJECT SPECIFICATIONS

Skill Level: Beginner
Quilt Size: 85" x 89¼"
Block Size: 4¼" x 4¼"
Number of Blocks: 210

Nine-Patch Squared
4¼" x 4¼" Block
Make 210

MATERIALS

- 1½ yards total white prints
- 1¾ yards total dark prints
- 2⅔ yards muslin
- 4⅜ yards red/white check
- Backing 91" x 96"
- Batting 91" x 96"
- Neutral-color all-purpose thread
- Quilting thread
- Basic sewing tools and supplies

Project Notes

If using scraps, note that in the antique quilt, one same-fabric dark is used in a block to create the Nine-Patch unit. The pieces for this quilt were cut using templates, and it was hand-pieced, making it easy to plan cutting using scraps.

When using rotary-cutting methods with whole strips subcut into units, it is easier to buy yardage to complete the units. It is possible to cut fabric-width strips of a variety of dark and light fabrics, but if you want to emulate the look of the antique, select same-fabric units to construct the Nine-Patch units.

This will probably mean that you will stitch more strip sets than needed and will have leftover segments. These may be used to make matching pillows or pillowcases.

Cutting

1. Cut a total of (31) 1½" by fabric width A strips white prints.

2. Cut a total of (38) 1½" by fabric width B strips dark prints.

3. Cut (30) 3" by fabric width strips muslin; subcut strips into (420) 3" squares. Cut each square in half on one diagonal to make 840 C triangles.

4. Cut (27) 4¾" by fabric width strips red/white check; subcut strips into (210) 4¾" D squares.

5. Cut nine 2¼" by fabric width strips red/white check for binding.

Completing the Blocks

1. Stitch an A strip between two B strips with right sides together along length to make a strip set; repeat for 15 B-A-B strip sets. Press seams toward B strips.

2. Repeat step 1 with a B strip between two A strips to complete eight A-B-A strip sets; press seams toward B strips.

3. Subcut the A-B-A strip sets into (210) 1½" A units and the B-A-B strip sets into (420) 1½" B units referring to Figure 1.

Figure 1

4. To complete one block, stitch an A unit between two B units to complete an A-B unit as shown in Figure 2; press seams away from the A unit.

Figure 2

5. Stitch a C triangle to opposite sides of the A-B unit; trim seams to ¼" and press seams toward C. Repeat on the remaining sides of the A-B unit to complete one block as shown in Figure 3. Press seams toward C.

Figure 3

6. Repeat steps 4 and 5 to make 210 blocks.

Completing the Quilt

1. Arrange and join 10 blocks with 10 D squares to make a row; press seams toward D. Repeat to make 21 rows.

2. Join the rows referring to the Placement Diagram to complete the pieced center; press seams in one direction.

3. Layer, quilt and bind referring to Finishing Your Quilt on page 176. ■

Nine-Patch Squared
Placement Diagram 85" x 87¼"

Sashed Pinwheels Bed Runner

Borrowed from an antique quilt in the designer's collection, this color scheme and block design translate well to any modern bedroom.

DESIGN BY SANDRA L. HATCH

PROJECT SPECIFICATIONS

Skill Level: Beginner
Bed Runner Size: 75½" x 21½"
Block Size: 9½" x 9½"
Number of Blocks: 5

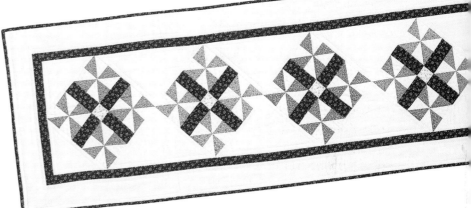

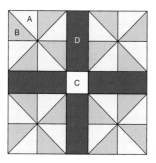

Sashed Pinwheels
9½" x 9½" Block
Make 5

MATERIALS

Note: On sample project, same-fabric B squares were used in one block; eight B squares of same fabric are needed for one block.

- (40) 2⅞" B squares assorted pink prints
- (5) 2" C squares white shirting stripe
- ⅜ yard white-with-pink print
- ⅞ yard navy print
- 1⅜ yards muslin
- Backing 82" x 28"
- Batting 82" x 28"
- All-purpose thread to match fabrics
- Quilting thread
- Basic sewing tools and supplies

Cutting

1. Cut three 2⅞" by fabric width strips white-with-pink print; subcut strips into (40) 2⅞" A squares.

2. Cut two 7⅝" squares muslin; cut each square in half on one diagonal to make four F triangles.

3. Cut two 14⅝" squares muslin; cut each square on both diagonals to make eight G triangles.

4. Cut four 3½" by fabric width strips muslin. Join two strips on short ends to make one long strip; press seam open. Repeat to make two strips; subcut each strip into a 3½" x 70" J strip.

5. Cut two 3½" x 22" K strips muslin.

6. Cut one 4½" by fabric width strip navy print; subcut strip into (20) 2" x 4½" D rectangles.

7. Cut four 1½" by fabric width strips navy print. Join strips on short ends to make one long strip; press seams open. Subcut strip into two 1½" x 68" H strips.

8. Cut two 1½" x 16" I strips navy print.

9. Cut five 2¼" by fabric width strips navy print for binding.

Completing the Blocks

1. Draw a diagonal line from corner to corner on the wrong side of each A square.

2. Place an A square right sides together with a B square; stitch ¼" on each side of the marked line on A as shown in Figure 1. Repeat for all A and B squares.

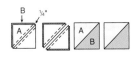

Figure 1

3. Cut the stitched units apart on the marked lines to complete 80 A-B units, again referring to Figure 1; open and press seams toward B.

4. To complete one block, select 16 same-fabric A-B units.

5. Join two A-B units to make an A-B row as shown in Figure 2; press seam in one direction. Repeat to make two rows.

Figure 2

6. Join the two A-B rows to complete a pinwheel unit as shown in Figure 3; press seam in one direction. Repeat to make two pinwheel units and two reversed pinwheel units, again referring to Figure 3.

Figure 3

7. Join one each pinwheel and reversed pinwheel units with D to make a pinwheel row as shown in

Figure 4; press seams toward D. Repeat to make two rows.

Figure 4

8. Join two D pieces with C to make the center row as shown in Figure 5; press seams toward D.

Figure 5

9. Sew the center row between the two pinwheel rows to complete one Sashed Pinwheels block referring to the block drawing; press seams toward the center row.

10. Repeat steps 4–9 to complete 5 blocks.

Completing the Bed Runner

1. Arrange the pieced blocks with the F and G triangles and join to complete the pieced center as shown in Figure 6; press seams toward F and G.

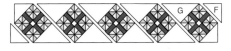

Figure 6

2. Sew an H strip to opposite long sides and I strips to each end of the pieced center; press seams toward H and I strips.

3. Sew a J strip to opposite long sides and K strips to each end to complete the pieced top; press seams toward J and K strips.

4. Layer, quilt and bind referring to Finishing Your Quilt on page 176. ■

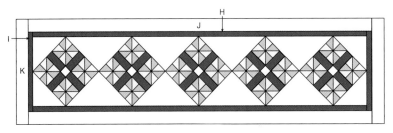

Sashed Pinwheels Bed Runner
Placement Diagram 75½" x 21½"

Reunion

A red floral adds versatility to a quilt that could be used to celebrate Christmas or the Fourth of July.

DESIGN BY MARIA UMHEY

PROJECT SPECIFICATIONS

Skill Level: Intermediate
Quilt Size: 81¾" x 81¾"
Block Size: 9" x 9"
Number of Blocks: 41

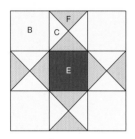

Reverse Ohio Star
9" x 9" Block
Make 16

Ohio Star
9" x 9" Block
Make 25

MATERIALS

- ¼ yard each 5 medium to dark blue prints
- 1 yard navy print
- 1½ yards gold print
- 2⅓ yards red floral
- 2¾ yards cream tonal
- Backing 88" x 88"
- Batting 88" x 88"
- Neutral-color all-purpose thread
- Quilting thread
- Basic sewing tools and supplies

Cutting

1. Cut a total of (25) 3½" A squares from the medium to dark blue and navy prints.

2. Cut two 4¼" squares to match each of the A squares; cut each square on both diagonals to make eight D triangles to match each A square. Total number of D triangles is 200.

3. Cut nine 2¼" by fabric width strips navy print for binding.

4. Cut (14) 3½" by fabric width strips cream tonal; subcut strips into (164) 3½" B squares.

5. Cut (10) 4¼" by fabric width strips cream tonal; subcut strips into (82) 4¼" squares. Cut each square on both diagonals to make 328 C triangles.

6. Cut four 4¼" by fabric width strips gold print; subcut strips into (32) 4¼" squares. Cut each square on both diagonals to make 128 F triangles.

7. Cut seven 3½" by fabric width strips gold print. Join strips on short ends to make one long strip; press seams open. Subcut strip into two 3½" x 64¼" I strips and two 3½" x 70¼" J strips.

8. Cut one 6½" by fabric width strip gold print; subcut strip into four 6½" L squares.

9. Cut two 3½" by fabric width strips red floral; subcut strips into (16) 3½" E squares.

10. Cut four 6½" x 70¼" K strips along the length of the remaining red floral.

11. Cut one 14"-wide strip along the length of the remaining red floral; subcut strip into four 14" G squares and two 7¼" H squares. Cut each G square on both diagonals to make 16 G triangles. Cut each H square in half on one diagonal to make four H triangles.

Completing the Ohio Star Blocks

1. To complete one Ohio Star block, sew C to D as shown in Figure 1; press seam toward D. Repeat to make eight matching C-D units.

Figure 1

2. Join two C-D units as shown in Figure 2 to make a side unit; press seam in one direction. Repeat to make four side units.

Figure 2

3. Sew a side unit to opposite sides of a matching A square to make the center row as shown in Figure 3; press seams toward A.

Figure 3

4. Sew B to the D sides of the remaining side units to make a top and bottom row as shown in Figure 4; press seams toward B.

Figure 4

5. Sew the top and bottom rows to the center row referring to the block drawing to complete one Ohio Star block; press seams away from the center row.

6. Repeat steps 1–5 to complete 25 blocks.

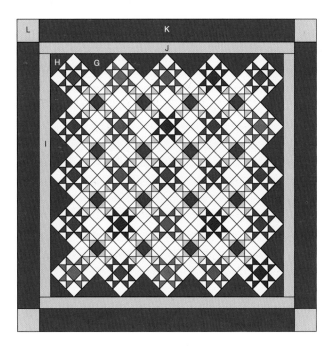

Reunion
Placement Diagram 81³⁄₄" x 81³⁄₄"

Completing the Reverse Ohio Star Blocks

1. Complete 16 Reverse Ohio Star blocks, referring to Completing the Ohio Star Blocks, substituting E for A and F for D and referring to Figure 5 for piecing C-F side units and to Figure 6 for completing rows.

Figure 5   **Figure 6**

Completing the Quilt

1. Arrange the pieced blocks in diagonal rows with G and H triangles referring to Figure 7; join to make rows. Press seams toward the Ohio Star blocks.

Figure 7

2. Join the rows to complete the pieced center; press seams in one direction.

3. Sew I strips to opposite sides and J strips to the remaining sides of the pieced center; press seams toward I and J strips.

4. Sew a K strip to opposite sides of the pieced center; press seams toward K strips. Sew an L square to each end of the remaining K strips; press seams toward K. Sew a K-L strip to the remaining sides of the pieced center to complete the top; press seams toward K-L strips.

5. Layer, quilt and bind referring to Finishing Your Quilt on page 176. ∎

Got the Blues

Collect your dark and light scraps to make a striking bed-size quilt.

DESIGN BY KARLA SCHULZ

PROJECT SPECIFICATIONS

Skill Level: Beginner
Quilt Size: 84" x 96"
Block Size: 12" x 12"
Number of Blocks: 56

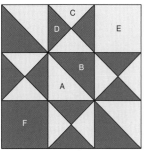

Split Star
12" x 12" Block
Make 28

Log Cabin
12" x 12" Block
Make 28

MATERIALS

- Assorted navy scraps
- Assorted cream/white scraps
- ½ yard navy print
- ¾ yard navy tonal
- Backing 92" x 104"
- Batting 92" x 104"
- All-purpose thread to match fabrics
- Quilting thread
- Basic sewing tools and supplies

Cutting

1. Cut one 4½" F square and two each 5¼" D squares and 4⅞" B squares from matching navy scraps to make a set.

2. Cut each B square in half on one diagonal to make 4 B triangles, discard one. Cut each D square on both diagonals to make 8 D triangles.

3. Repeat steps 1 and 2 to make 28 sets of matching B and D triangles, and F squares.

4. Cut 2"-wide strips from a variety of the remaining navy scraps for dark Log Cabin strips.

5. Cut one 4½" E square and two each 5¼" C and 4⅞" A squares from matching cream/white scraps to make a set.

6. Cut each C square on both diagonals to make 8 C triangles. Cut each A square in half on one diagonal to make four A triangles; discard one.

7. Repeat steps 5 and 6 to make 28 sets of matching A and C triangles, and E squares.

8. Cut 2"-wide strips from a variety of the remaining cream/white scraps for light Log Cabin strips.

9. Cut three 3½" by fabric width navy print strips; subcut strips into (28) 3½" G squares.

10. Cut nine 2½" by fabric width navy tonal strips for binding.

Completing the Log Cabin Blocks

1. Stitch a 2"-wide light strip (No. 1) to one side of a G square as shown in Figure 1; press seam toward strip.

Figure 1   **Figure 2**

2. Trim the strip even with G as shown in Figure 2.

3. Repeat steps 1 and 2 with light strip (No. 2) and Nos. 3 and 4 (2"-wide) dark strips to complete one round of strips on G as shown in Figure 3.

Figure 3

4. Continue adding light and dark strips in numerical order in the same manner until there are three light strips on two sides and three dark strips on the remaining sides of G to complete one Log Cabin block referring to the block drawing; press seams toward strips.

5. Repeat steps 1–4 to complete 28 Log Cabin blocks.

Completing the Split Star Blocks

1. To complete one Split Star block, select one matching set of B, D and F pieces and one matching set of A, C and E pieces.

2. Stitch A to B along the diagonal; press seam toward B. Repeat to make three A-B units.

3. Stitch C to D on a short side to make a C-D unit as shown in Figure 4; press seam toward D. Repeat to make eight C-D units.

Make 8

Make 4

Figure 4   **Figure 5**

4. Join two C-D units to make a C-D square as shown in Figure 5; press seam in one direction. Repeat to make four C-D squares.

5. Join one A-B unit with one each C-D and E square to make the top row as shown in Figure 6; press seams away from the C-D square.

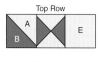

Top Row

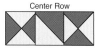

Center Row

Figure 6   **Figure 7**

6. Stitch an A-B unit between two C-D squares to make the center row as shown in Figure 7; press seams toward the A-B unit.

7. Stitch one each F and C-D square with an A-B unit to make the bottom row as shown in Figure 8; press seams away from C-D square.

Bottom Row

Figure 8

8. Join the rows to complete one Split Star block referring to the block drawing; press seams away from the center row.

9. Repeat steps 1–8 to complete 28 Split Star blocks.

Completing the Quilt

1. Arrange and join three Log Cabin blocks with four Split Star blocks to make an X row as shown in Figure 9; press seams toward Log Cabin blocks. Repeat to make four X rows.

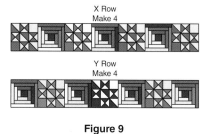

X Row
Make 4

Y Row
Make 4

Figure 9

2. Join three Split Star blocks with four Log Cabin blocks to make a Y row, again referring to Figure 9; press seams toward Log Cabin blocks. Repeat to make four Y rows.

3. Join the X and Y rows referring to the Placement Diagram to complete the pieced top; press seams in one direction.

4. Layer, quilt and bind referring to Finishing Your Quilt on page 176. ■

Got the Blues
Placement Diagram 84" x 96"

Cabin in the Woods

Earth-tone tonals add warmth to this easy-to-stitch quilt.

DESIGN BY MICHELE CRAWFORD

PROJECT SPECIFICATIONS

Skill Level: Beginner
Quilt Size: 60" x 72"
Block Size: 12" x 12"
Number of Blocks: 20

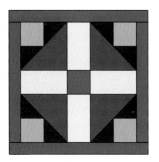

Cabin A
12" x 12" Block
Make 10

Cabin B
12" x 12" Block
Make 10

MATERIALS

- ½ yard medium green tonal
- ½ yard medium brown tonal
- ½ yard cream tonal
- ⅔ yard dark green tonal
- ⅔ yard tan tonal
- ¾ yard dark brown tonal
- 1⅛ yards red tonal
- 1⅛ yards gold tonal
- 1⅓ yards black solid
- Backing 68" x 80"
- Batting 68" x 80"
- All-purpose thread to match fabrics
- Quilting thread
- Basting spray
- Basic sewing tools and supplies

Cutting

1. Cut three 4½" by fabric width strips cream tonal. Subcut strips into (40) 2½" x 4½" A rectangles. Repeat with dark green tonal to make 40 H rectangles.

2. Cut one 2½" by fabric width strip red tonal; subcut strip into (10) 2½" B squares. Repeat with gold tonal to make 10 I squares.

3. Cut three 4⅞" by fabric width strips dark brown tonal; subcut strips into (20) 4⅞" squares. Cut each square on one diagonal to make 40 C triangles. Repeat with tan tonal to make 40 K triangles.

4. Cut six 2⅞" by fabric width strips black solid; subcut strips into (80) 2⅞" squares. Cut each square on one diagonal to make 160 D triangles.

5. Cut three 2½" by fabric width strips medium green tonal; subcut strips into (40) 2½" E squares. Repeat with medium brown tonal to make 40 J squares.

6. Cut one 10½" by fabric width strip red tonal; subcut strip into (20) 1½" x 10½" F strips. Repeat with gold tonal to make 20 L strips.

7. Cut one 12½" by fabric width strip red tonal; subcut strip into (20) 1½" x 12½" G strips. Repeat with gold tonal to make 20 M strips.

8. Cut seven 1½" by fabric width strips black solid. Join strips on short ends to make one long strip; press seams open. Subcut strip into two 1½" x 48½" N strips, two 1½" x 62½" O strips and eight 1½" x 5½" Q strips.

9. Cut two 3½" by fabric width P strips each tonal fabric except cream and tan.

10. Cut four 5½" R squares tan tonal.

11. Cut seven 2¼" by fabric width strips black solid for binding.

Completing Cabin A Blocks

1. To complete one Cabin A block, stitch A to opposite sides of B to complete the center row; press seams toward A.

2. Stitch D to two adjacent sides of E and add C to make a corner unit as shown in Figure 1; press seams toward D and C. Repeat for four corner units.

Figure 1

3. Join two corner units with A to make a top row as shown in Figure 2; press seams toward A. Repeat for bottom row.

Figure 2

4. Stitch the center row between the top and bottom rows referring to Figure 3; press seams toward the center row.

Figure 3

5. Stitch an F strip to opposite sides and a G strip to the top and bottom of the pieced unit as shown in Figure 4 to complete one block; press seams toward F and G.

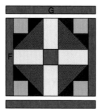

Figure 4

6. Repeat steps 1–5 to make 10 Cabin A blocks.

Completing Cabin B Blocks

1. To complete one Cabin B block, stitch H to opposite sides of I to complete the center row; press seams toward H.

2. Stitch D to two adjacent sides of J and add K to make a corner unit as shown in Figure 5; press seams toward D and K. Repeat to make four corner units.

Figure 5

3. Join two corner units with H to make a top row as shown in Figure 6; press seams toward H. Repeat to make bottom row.

Figure 6

4. Stitch the center row between the top and bottom rows referring to Figure 7; press seams toward the center row.

Figure 7

5. Stitch an L strip to the top and bottom, and an M strip to opposite sides of the pieced unit, as shown in Figure 8, to complete one block; press seams toward L and M.

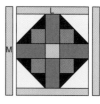

Figure 8

6. Repeat steps 1–5 to make 10 Cabin B blocks.

Completing the Top

1. Referring to the Placement Diagram for positioning of blocks, join two each Cabin A and Cabin B blocks to make a row, alternating blocks; press seams toward A blocks. Repeat to make five rows.

2. Join the rows, again referring to the Placement Diagram for positioning of rows.

3. Stitch an N strip to the top and bottom of the pieced center; press seams toward N strips.

4. Stitch an O strip to opposite sides of the pieced center; press seams toward O strips.

5. Join one P strip each color with right sides together along length referring to Figure 9 for color order; press seams in one direction. Repeat to make two strip sets. Subcut strip sets into (12) 5½" P units, again referring to Figure 9.

Figure 9

6. Join three P units as shown in Figure 10; repeat to make four P strips. Press seams in one direction. Remove the gold and medium brown P pieces from one end of two strips for two short P strips, again referring to Figure 10.

Figure 10

7. Stitch a Q strip to each end of the two short P strips as shown in Figure 11; press seams toward Q strips.

Figure 11

8. Stitch the short P-Q strips to the top and bottom of the pieced center referring to the Placement Diagram for positioning of strips.

9. Stitch the gold and medium brown P pieces removed from the strips in step 6 to the medium green end of each of the remaining two strips as shown in Figure 12 to make two long P strips; press seams in one direction.

Figure 12

10. Stitch a Q strip and an R square to each end of each long P strip as shown in Figure 13; press seams toward Q. Stitch these strips to opposite long sides of the pieced center to complete the pieced top referring to the Placement Diagram for positioning of strips; press seams toward strips.

Figure 13

11. Layer, quilt and bind referring to Finishing Your Quilt on page 176. ■

Cabin in the Woods
Placement Diagram 60" x 72"

Square Dance

The secondary design created when blocks are joined becomes the dominant feature of this quilt.

DESIGN BY TOBY LISCHKO

PROJECT SPECIFICATIONS

Skill Level: Intermediate
Quilt Size: 50" x 50"
Block Size: 10" x 10"
Number of Blocks: 16

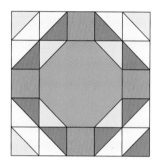

Corner
10" x 10" Block
Make 4

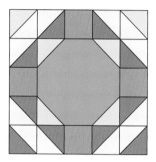

Edge
10" x 10" Block
Make 8

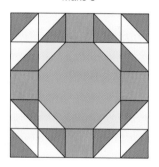

Center
10" x 10" Block
Make 4

MATERIALS

- ⅜ yard green print
- ½ yard rust tonal
- ⅔ yard gold tonal
- ¾ yard red print
- 1 yard floral print
- 1 yard yellow print
- 1¼ yards floral stripe
- Backing 56" x 56"
- Batting 56" x 56"
- Neutral-color all-purpose thread
- Quilting thread
- Basic sewing tools and supplies

Cutting

1. Cut four 2½" by fabric width strips green print; subcut strips into (64) 2½" C squares.

2. Cut six 2¼" by fabric width strips rust tonal for binding.

3. Cut four 2½" by fabric width strips gold tonal; subcut strips into (64) 2½" B squares.

4. Cut one 2⅞" by fabric width strip gold tonal; subcut strip into (14) 2⅞" F squares. Cut each square on one diagonal to make 28 F triangles.

5. Cut four 1½" x 40½" G strips gold tonal.

6. Cut six 2⅞" by fabric width strips red print; subcut strips into (82) 2⅞" D squares. Cut each square on one diagonal to make 164 D triangles.

7. Cut four 1" x 40½" H strips red print.

8. Cut three 6½" by fabric width strips floral print; subcut strips into (16) 6½" A squares.

9. Cut two 3" by fabric width strips floral print; subcut strips into (16) 3" J squares.

10. Cut seven 2⅞" by fabric width strips yellow print; subcut strips into (96) 2⅞" E squares. Cut each square on one diagonal to make 192 E triangles.

11. Cut one 5½" by fabric width strip yellow print; subcut four 5½" K squares.

12. Cut four 4" x 40½" I strips along the length of floral stripe.

Completing the Blocks

1. Draw a line from corner to corner on the wrong side of each B square.

2. Place a B square on each corner of A referring to Figure 1; stitch on the marked line.

Figure 1

3. Trim excess ¼" from seam and press B to the right side to complete an A-B unit as shown in Figure 2; repeat to make 16 A-B units.

Figure 2

4. Stitch D to E along the diagonal to make a D-E unit; repeat for 164 D-E units. Press seams toward D.

5. Repeat step 4 to complete 28 E-F units; press seams toward E.

6. Arrange D-E and E-F units with C to make rows referring to Figure 3; press seams toward C.

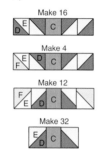

Figure 3

Square Dance
Placement Diagram 50" x 50"

7. Join the stitched rows with the A-B units to complete the blocks as shown in Figure 4; press seams in one direction.

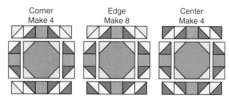

Figure 4

Completing the Top

1. Arrange the blocks in rows referring to Figure 5 for positioning. Join blocks in rows; press seams in adjacent rows in opposite directions.

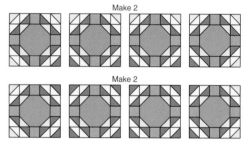

Figure 5

2. Join rows to complete the pieced center referring to the Placement Diagram. Press seams in one direction.

3. Stitch a G strip to an H strip to an I strip with right sides together along length; press seams toward G and I strips.

4. Stitch a G-H-I strip to opposite sides of the pieced center with G on the inside; press seams toward strips.

5. Draw a diagonal line from corner to corner on the wrong side of each J square.

6. Stitch J to each corner of K as in steps 2 and 3 for Completing the Blocks; repeat to make four J-K units.

7. Stitch a J-K unit to each end of each remaining G-H-I strip; press seam toward J-K units.

8. Stitch strips to the remaining sides of the pieced center; press seams toward strips.

9. Layer, quilt and bind referring to Finishing Your Quilt on page 176. ■

Romancing the Nines

Romance is a state of mind. These Nine-Patch variations will inspire you to create a mood of romance at home or at the beach. A quilt can create a sense of belonging and comfort.

Bloomin' Topper

The trick to this topper is in the placement. It's a great project to use up leftover stash.

DESIGN BY CAROLYN S. VAGTS FOR THE VILLAGE PATTERN CO.

PROJECT SPECIFICATIONS

Skill Level: Beginner
Quilt Size: 36" x 36"
Block Size: 6" x 6"
Number of Blocks: 36

Block 1
6" x 6" Block
Make 10

Block 2
6" x 6" Block
Make 10

Block 3
6" x 6" Block
Make 2

Block 4
6" x 6" Block
Make 4

Block 5
6" x 6" Block
Make 4

Block 6
6" x 6" Block
Make 2

Block 7
6" x 6" Block
Make 2

Block 8
6" x 6" Block
Make 2

MATERIALS

Note: *If using scraps or Jelly Roll precuts instead of yardage, refer to cutting instructions for total number of squares to cut from each color.*

- ¼ yard each pale green, multi-pastel, tan/blue and dark tan batiks
- ⅜ yard dark brown batik
- ⅝ yard light brown batik
- ⅔ yard total assorted medium aqua batiks
- Backing 44" x 44"
- Batting 44" x 44"
- Neutral-color all-purpose thread
- Quilting thread
- Basic sewing tools and supplies

Cutting

1. Cut two 2½" by fabric width pale green batik strips; subcut strips into (18) 2½" A squares.

2. Cut two 2½" by fabric width multi-pastel batik strips; subcut strips into (32) 2½" B squares.

3. Cut two 2½" by fabric width tan/blue batik strips; subcut strips into (32) 2½" C squares.

4. Cut two 2½" by fabric width dark tan batik strips; subcut strips into (30) 2½" F squares.

5. Cut four 2½" by fabric width dark brown batik strips; subcut strips into (60) 2½" G squares.

6. Cut two 2½" by fabric width light brown batik strips; subcut strips into (30) 2½" E squares.

7. Cut four 2½" by fabric width light brown batik strips for binding.

8. Cut eight 2½" by fabric width assorted medium aqua batik strips; subcut strips into (122) 2½" D squares.

Completing the Blocks

1. To complete Block 1, select three each D and G, one E and two F squares. Sew one E between two G squares to make the top row of Block 1 as shown in Figure 1. Press seams to one side.

Figure 1

2. Sew a G square between two D squares to make the center row as shown in Figure 2. Press seams in opposite direction of top row.

Figure 2

3. Sew a D square between two F squares to make the bottom row of Block 1 as shown in Figure 3. Press seams in same direction of top row. Sew rows together referring to Block 1 drawing; press seams in one direction.

Figure 3

4. Repeat steps 1–3 to make 10 of Block 1.

5. To make Blocks 2–8, refer to block drawings for type and number of squares and for placement. Referring to steps 1–3 above, stitch the squares in rows and then stitch the rows into a block. Make 10 of Block 2, four each of Blocks 4 and 5, and two each of Blocks 3 and 6–8 as noted on block drawings.

Completing the Quilt

1. Referring to Figure 4, arrange and stitch three each Blocks 1 and 2 together to make row 1; press seams toward the right.

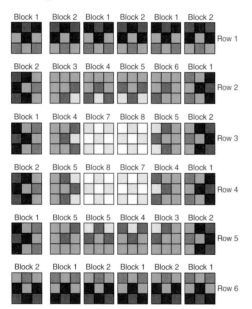

Figure 4

2. Complete rows 2–6, again referring to Figure 4 for positioning and arrangement of blocks for each row. Press seams in opposite directions row to row. **Note:** *Pay close attention to block orientation. Rows 4–6 are mirror images of rows 1–3.*

3. Sew rows together in numerical order. Press seams in one direction.

4. Layer, quilt and bind referring to Finishing Your Quilt on page 176. ■

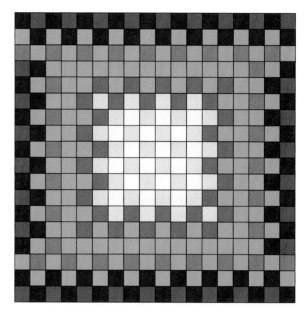

Blooming Topper
Placement Diagram 36" x 36"

Blizzard in Blue Bed Quilt

Make this holiday bed quilt using shades of blue for a change of pace this year.

DESIGN BY KARLA SCHULZ

PROJECT SPECIFICATIONS

Skill Level: Intermediate
Quilt Size: 98¾" x 98¾"
Block Size: 26¼" x 26¼"
Number of Blocks: 9

Blizzard in Blue
26¼" x 26¼" Block
Make 9

MATERIALS

- 1¼ yards blue snowflake print
- 1⅓ yards blue holly print
- 1½ yards blue stripe
- 1⅞ yards blue poinsettia print
- 2 yards navy tonal
- 2⅜ yards white solid
- 3¼ yards gray snowflake print
- Backing 105" x 105"
- Batting 105" x 105"
- Neutral-color all-purpose thread
- Quilting thread
- Basic sewing tools and supplies

Cutting

1. Cut (10) 2¾" by fabric width blue snowflake print strips; subcut strips into (144) 2¾" squares. Cut each square in half on one diagonal to make 288 L triangles

2. Cut five 2⅜" by fabric width blue snowflake print strips; subcut strips into (72) 2⅜" P squares.

3. Cut six 3⅛" by fabric width blue holly print strips; subcut strips into (72) 3⅛" squares. Cut each square in half on one diagonal to make 144 D triangles.

4. Cut three 2⅜" by fabric width blue holly print strips; subcut strips into (36) 2⅜" T squares.

5. Cut six 3" by fabric width blue holly print strips; subcut strips into (72) 3" squares. Cut each square in half on one diagonal to make 144 H triangles.

6. Cut four 4¼" by fabric width blue stripe strips; subcut strips into (36) 4¼" R squares.

7. Cut three 2⅜" by fabric width blue stripe strips; subcut strips into (36) 2⅜" S squares.

8. Cut nine 2½" by fabric width blue stripe W/X strips.

9. Cut nine 6½" by fabric width blue poinsettia print Y/Z strips.

10. Cut four 4" by fabric width navy tonal strips; subcut strips into (36) 4" squares. Cut each square in half on one diagonal to make 72 O triangles.

11. Cut five 2⅜" by fabric width navy tonal strips; subcut strips into (72) 2⅜" Q squares.

12. Cut three 2¾" by fabric width navy tonal strips; subcut strips into (36) 2¾" squares. Cut each square in half on one diagonal to make 72 N triangles.

13. Cut (10) 2¼" by fabric width navy tonal strips for binding.

14. Cut two 7½" by fabric width white solid strips; subcut strips into nine 7½" squares. Cut each square on both diagonals to make 36 E triangles.

15. Cut five 4¾" by fabric width white solid strips; subcut strips into (36) 4¾" J squares.

16. Cut three 3" by fabric width white solid strips; subcut strips into (36) 3" squares. Cut each square in half on one diagonal to make 72 I triangles.

17. Cut (12) 2¾" by fabric width white solid strips; subcut strips into (180) 2¾" squares. Cut each square in half on one diagonal to make 360 K triangles.

18. Cut two 6¾" by fabric width gray snowflake print strips; subcut strips into nine 6¾" A squares.

19. Cut three 2¾" by fabric width gray snowflake print strips; subcut strips into (36) 2¾" B squares.

20. Cut three 3⅛" by fabric width gray snowflake print strips; subcut strips into (36) 3⅛" squares. Cut each square in half on one diagonal to make 72 C triangles.

21. Cut three 2⅝" by fabric width gray snowflake print strips; subcut strips into (36) 2⅝" F squares.

22. Cut three 3" by fabric width gray snowflake print strips; subcut strips into (36) 3" squares. Cut each square in half on one diagonal to make 72 G triangles.

23. Cut five 8" by fabric width gray snowflake print strips; subcut strips into (72) 2⅜" x 8" M rectangles.

24. Cut eight 2½" by fabric width gray snowflake U/V print strips.

Completing the Blocks

1. Sew C to D on the diagonal to make a C-D unit as shown in Figure 1; press seam toward D. Repeat to make 72 C-D units.

Make 72 Make 72 Make 72 Make 288 Make 72

Figure 1

2. Sew G to H on the diagonal to make a G-H unit, again referring to Figure 1; press seam toward H. Repeat to make 72 G-H units.

3. Sew H to I on the diagonal to make an H-I unit, again referring to Figure 1; press seam toward H. Repeat to make 72 H-I units.

4. Sew K to L on the diagonal to make a K-L unit, again referring to Figure 1; press seam toward L. Repeat to make 288 K-L units.

5. Sew K to N on the diagonal to make a K-N unit, again referring to Figure 1; press seam toward N. Repeat to make 72 K-N units.

6. Mark a diagonal line from corner to corner on the wrong side of each P and Q square.

7. Referring to Figure 2, place a P square right sides together on one corner of R; stitch on the marked line. Trim seam to ¼" and press P to the right side.

Figure 2

8. Repeat step 7 with another P square and two Q squares to complete a P-Q-R unit as shown in Figure 3. Repeat to make 36 P-Q-R units.

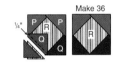

Figure 3

9. To complete one Blizzard in Blue block, sew D to the C side of one C-D unit as shown in Figure 4; repeat to make a reverse unit. Press seams toward D.

Figure 4

Figure 5

10. Sew B to the C-D-D unit as shown in Figure 5; press seam toward B.

11. Sew E to the reverse C-D-D unit and add the C-D-D-B unit as shown in Figure 6; press seams away from E.

Figure 6   **Figure 7**

12. Sew O to the pieced unit to complete a side unit as shown in Figure 7; press seams toward O. Repeat steps 9–12 to make four side units.

13. Join one G-H and one H-I unit as shown in Figure 8; repeat to make a reverse G-H-I unit. Press seams in one direction.

Figure 8

14. Sew F to the G-H-I unit and J to the reverse G-H-I unit as shown in Figure 9; press seams toward F and J.

Figure 9

15. Join the two units to complete a corner unit, again referring to Figure 9; press seam open. Repeat steps 13–15 to make four corner units.

16. Sew a side unit to opposite sides of A to make the center row as shown in Figure 10; press seams toward A.

Figure 10

17. Sew a side unit between two corner units to make a side row as shown in Figure 11; press seams toward the corner units. Repeat to make two side rows.

Figure 11

18. Sew a side row to opposite sides of the center row to complete the block center as shown in Figure 12; press seams toward the center row.

Figure 12

19. Join four K-L units and add M to make a side section as shown in Figure 13; press seams open. Repeat to make four side sections and four reverse side sections.

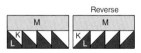

Figure 13

20. Sew T to K-N and S to K-N as shown in Figure 14; press seams toward S and T. Repeat to make four each K-N-S and K-N-T units.

Figure 14

21. Join one each K-N-S and K-N-T units to complete a corner section, again referring to Figure 14; press seam open. Repeat to make four corner units.

22. Join a side section and reverse side section with a P-Q-R unit to make a side strip as shown in Figure 15; press seams open. Repeat to make four side strips.

Figure 15

23. Sew a side strip to opposite sides of the block center; press seams away from the block center.

24. Sew a corner unit to each end of each remaining side section as shown in Figure 16; press seams open.

Figure 16

25. Sew a side section/corner unit to the remaining sides of the block center to complete the block; press seams away from the block center.

26. Repeat steps 9–25 to complete nine Blizzard in Blue blocks.

Completing the Bed Quilt

1. Join three Blizzard in Blue blocks to make a row; press seams in one direction. Repeat to make three rows.

2. Join the rows, alternating the direction of the pressed seams, to complete the pieced center; press seams in one direction.

3. Join the U/V strips with right sides together on short ends to make one long strip; press seams open. Subcut strip into two 2½ x 79¼" U strips and two 2½ x 83¼" V strips.

4. Sew U strips to opposite sides and V strips to the top and bottom of the pieced center; press seams toward U and V strips.

5. Join the W/X strips with right sides together on short ends to make one long strip; press seams open. Subcut strip into two 2½" x 83¼" W strips and two 2½" x 87¼" X strips.

6. Sew W strips to opposite sides and X strips to the top and bottom of the pieced center; press seams toward W and X strips.

7. Join the Y/Z strips with right sides together on short ends to make one long strip; press seams open. Subcut strip into two 6½" x 87¼" Y strips and two 6½" x 99¼" Z strips.

8. Sew Y strips to opposite sides and Z strips to the top and bottom of the pieced center; press seams toward Y and Z strips.

9. Layer, quilt and bind referring to Finishing Your Quilt on page 176. ∎

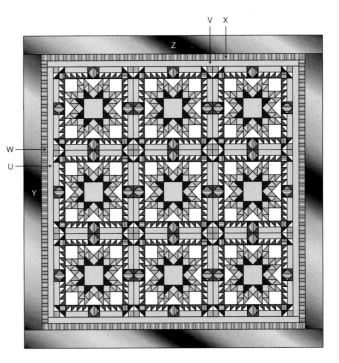

Blizzard in Blue Bed Quilt
Placement Diagram 98¾" x 98¾"

Toile Wreaths

Randomly cut toile for the block centers and backgrounds come together for an allover, coordinated look.

DESIGN BY SUE HARVEY & SANDY BOOBAR FOR PINE TREE COUNTRY QUILTS & KITS

PROJECT SPECIFICATIONS

Skill Level: Intermediate
Quilt Size: 104" x 104"
Block Size: 18" x 18"
Number of Blocks: 16

MATERIALS

Toile Wreath
18" x 18" Block
Make 16

- 2⅝ yards blue stripe
- 3¼ yards navy tonal
- 3¼ yards blue toile
- 3⅔ yards blue floral
- Backing 110" x 110"
- Batting 110" x 110"
- All-purpose thread to match fabrics
- Hand- or machine-quilting thread
- Basic sewing tools and supplies

Cutting

1. Cut three 6½" by fabric width strips blue toile; subcut strips into (16) 6½" A squares.

2. Cut four 6½" by fabric width strips blue toile; subcut strips into (64) 2½" x 6½" C rectangles.

3. Cut eight 2½" by fabric width strips blue toile; subcut strips into (128) 2½" D squares.

4. Cut six 6⅞" by fabric width strips blue toile; subcut strips into (32) 6⅞" F squares.

5. Cut (16) 2½" by fabric width strips navy tonal; subcut strips into (256) 2½" B squares.

6. Cut one 4½" by fabric width strip navy tonal; subcut strip into four 4½" K squares.

7. Cut (16) 2½" by fabric width strips navy tonal for H/I and L/M borders.

8. Cut (11) 2¼" by fabric width strips navy tonal for binding.

9. Cut six 6⅞" by fabric width strips blue floral; subcut strips into (32) 6⅞" G squares.

10. Cut (10) 8½" by fabric width strips blue floral for N/O borders.

11. Cut eight 6½" by fabric width strips blue stripe; subcut strips into (128) 2½" x 6½" E rectangles.

12. Cut eight 4½" by fabric width strips blue stripe for J borders.

Piecing the Blocks

1. Draw a diagonal line from corner to corner on the wrong side of each B, D and F square.

2. Place a B square right sides together on each corner of A as shown in Figure 1; stitch on the marked lines, trim seam allowances to ¼" and press B open to complete a center unit, again referring to Figure 1. Repeat to make 16 center units.

Figure 1

3. Repeat step 2 with a D square on one end of E and a B square on the remaining end of E to complete 64 each B-D-E and reversed B-D-E units as shown in Figure 2.

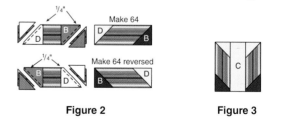

Figure 2   **Figure 3**

4. Sew a B-D-E unit and a reversed B-D-E unit to opposite sides of C to make a side unit as shown in Figure 3; press seams toward C. Repeat to make 64 side units.

5. Place F right sides together with G; stitch ¼" on each side of the marked line, cut apart on the marked line and press seams toward G to complete two F-G units as shown in Figure 4. Repeat to make 64 F-G units.

Figure 4

6. Place a B square right sides together on the F corner of an F-G unit; stitch, trim and press as in step 2 and referring to Figure 5 to complete one corner unit. Repeat to make 64 corner units.

Figure 5

7. To complete one block, sew a center unit between two side units to complete a center row as shown in Figure 6; press seams toward the side units.

Figure 6

8. Sew a side unit between two corner units to make a side row, again referring to Figure 6; press seams toward the side unit. Repeat for two rows.

9. Sew the center row between the two side rows to complete one Toile Wreath block referring to the block drawing for positioning of rows; press seams toward the side rows.

10. Repeat steps 7–9 to make 16 blocks.

Completing the Quilt

1. Join four blocks to make a row; press seams in one direction. Repeat for four rows.

2. Join the rows to complete the pieced center; press seams in one direction.

3. Join the H/I and L/M border strips on short ends to make a long strip; press seams in one direction. Subcut into two strips each 72½" (H), 76½" (I), 84½" (L) and 88½" (M).

4. Sew H to opposite sides and I to the remaining sides of the pieced center; press seams toward H and I strips.

5. Join the J strips on short ends to make a long strip; press seams in one direction. Subcut into four 76½" J strips.

6. Sew J to opposite sides of the pieced center; press seams toward J strips.

7. Sew K to each end of the remaining J strips; press seams toward J.

8. Sew a J-K strip to the remaining sides of the pieced center; press seams toward J-K strips.

9. Sew L to opposite sides and M to the remaining sides of the pieced center; press seams toward L and M strips.

10. Join the N/O border strips on short ends to make a long strip; press seams in one direction. Cut into two 88½" N strips and two 104½" O strips.

11. Sew N to opposite sides and O to the remaining sides of the pieced center to complete the top; press seams toward N and O strips.

12. Layer, quilt and bind referring to Finishing Your Quilt on page 176. ■

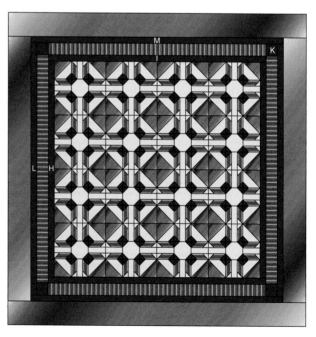

Toile Wreaths
Placement Diagram 104" x 104"

Dewdrops

Light to dark, left to right—this stunning quilt is easy to piece.

DESIGN BY CHLOE ANDERSON & COLLEEN REALE FOR TOADUSEW

PROJECT SPECIFICATIONS

Skill Level: Beginner
Quilt Size: 72" x 81"

PROJECT NOTES

The fabric collection used in this quilt was chosen because of the diverse prints, which created a perfect range for a watercolor quilt.

Fabrics that have many different shades and tones of one color that create movement within the same fabric would work well in this quilt. The two major color combinations that were used in the sample were blue/green and purple/pink. Using prints that offer a gradation from light to dark or from one color to another will give quilters a wealth of flexibility.

MATERIALS

- Blue/green tonals (approximately 4¼ yards total):
    ⅝ yard very light
    ¾ yard light
    1¾ yards medium
    1 yard dark
- Purple/pink tonals (approximately 3 yards total):
    ½ yard very light
    ½ yard light
    1 yard medium
    ⅔ yard dark
- ¾ yard blue tonal
- Backing 78" x 87"
- Batting 78" x 87"
- All-purpose thread to match fabrics
- Quilting thread
- Basic sewing tools and supplies

Cutting

Note: *If using scraps, cut the total number of squares indicated.*

1. Cut five 3½" by fabric width strips very light blue/green tonal; subcut strips into (54) 3½" A squares.

2. Cut six 3½" by fabric width strips light blue/green tonal; subcut strips into (63) 3½" B squares.

3. Cut (15) 3½" by fabric width strips medium blue/green tonal; subcut strips into (171) 3½" C squares.

4. Cut nine 3½" by fabric width strips dark blue/green tonal; subcut strips into (108) 3½" D squares.

5. Cut three 3½" by fabric width strips very light purple/pink tonal; subcut strips into (36) 3½" E squares.

6. Cut four 3½" by fabric width strips light purple/pink tonal; subcut strips into (45) 3½" F squares.

7. Cut nine 3½" by fabric width strips medium purple/pink tonal; subcut strips into (108) 3½" G squares.

8. Cut six 3½" by fabric width strips dark purple/pink tonal; subcut strips into (63) 3½" H squares.

9. Cut eight 2¼" by fabric width blue tonal strips for binding.

Completing the Nine-Patch Units

1. Select nine very light blue/green A squares; join three squares to make a row. Press seams in one direction. Repeat to make three rows.

2. Join the rows referring to Figure 1 to make an A unit; press seams as shown in Figure 2. **Note:** *The seams in all units are pressed as indicated by arrows in Figure 2.* Repeat to make six A units.

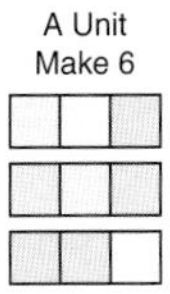

A Unit
Make 6

Figure 1

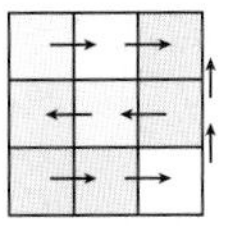

Figure 2

3. Repeat steps 1 and 2 with B squares to make seven B units as shown in Figure 3.

B Unit
Make 7

Figure 3

4. Repeat steps 1 and 2 with C squares to make 19 C units as shown in Figure 4.

C Unit
Make 19

Figure 4

5. Repeat steps 1 and 2 with D squares to make 12 D units as shown in Figure 5.

D Unit
Make 12

Figure 5

6. Repeat steps 1 and 2 with E squares to make four E units as shown in Figure 6.

E Unit
Make 4

Figure 6

7. Repeat steps 1 and 2 with F squares to make five F units as shown in Figure 7.

F Unit
Make 5

Figure 7

8. Repeat steps 1 and 2 with G squares to make 12 G units as shown in Figure 8.

G Unit
Make 12

Figure 8

H Unit
Make 7

Figure 9

9. Repeat steps 1 and 2 with H squares to make seven H units as shown in Figure 9.

Completing the Quilt

1. Arrange and join the pieced units in rows as shown in Figure 10. **Note:** *Turn the blocks within a row and from row to row as shown in Figure 11 so that pressing of seams are offset and will nest together to reduce bulk.*

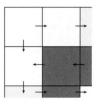

Figure 10   **Figure 11**

2. Arrange and join the rows, again referring to Figure 10 to complete the pieced top; press seams in one direction.

3. Staystitch ⅛" around the edges of the quilt before quilting to keep all seams intact for the quilting process.

4. Layer, quilt and bind referring to Finishing Your Quilt on page 176. ◼

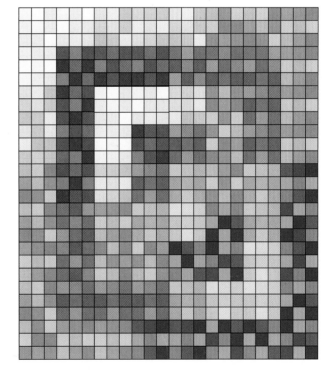

Dewdrops
Placement Diagram 72" x 81"

Romantic Heart

Rose clusters stand out as the focal point
in this lovely pieced quilt.

DESIGN BY LARISA KEY

PROJECT SPECIFICATIONS

Skill Level: Beginner
Quilt Size: 60" x 80"
Block Size: 10" x 10"
Number of Blocks: 39

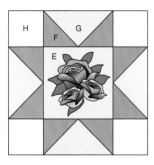

Rose Star
10" x 10" Block
Make 20

Nine-Patch Square
10" x 10" Block
Make 19

MATERIALS

- ⅝ yard each pink and blue tonals
- ⅝ yard white/blue toile
- ⅝ yard green petal print
- 1⅛ yards yellow print
- 1⅛ yards rose floral
- 1⅛ yards gold tonal
- 1⅝ yards blue petal print
- 1⅞ yards coordinating lengthwise stripe
- Backing 66" x 86"
- Batting 66" x 86"
- Neutral-color all-purpose thread
- Quilting thread
- Basic sewing tools and supplies

Cutting

1. Cut three 5½" by fabric width strips pink tonal; subcut strips into (19) 5½" A squares.

2. Cut six 3" by fabric width strips green petal print; subcut strips into (76) 3" B squares. Mark a diagonal line from corner to corner on the wrong side of each square.

3. Cut six 3" by fabric width C strips blue tonal.

4. Cut six 5½" by fabric width D strips gold tonal; subcut three strips into (38) 3" x 5½" D rectangles.

5. Fussy-cut (20) 5½" E squares rose floral.

6. Cut (12) 3" by fabric width strips blue petal print; subcut strips into (160) 3" F squares. Mark a diagonal line from corner to corner on the wrong side of each square.

7. Cut seven 2¼" by fabric width strips blue petal print for binding.

8. Cut six 5½" by fabric width strips yellow print; subcut strips into (80) 3" x 5½" G rectangles.

9. Cut six 3" by fabric width strips white/blue toile; subcut strips into (80) 3" H squares.

10. Cut two 5½" x 62" I strips and two 5½" x 42" J strips along the length of the coordinating lengthwise stripe.

Completing the Nine-Patch Square Blocks

1. Referring to Figure 1, place a B square on opposite corners of A; stitch on the marked lines. Trim seam allowances to ¼"; press B to the right side.

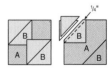

Figure 1

2. Repeat step 1 on the remaining corners of A to complete an A-B unit as shown in Figure 2. Repeat to make 19 A-B units.

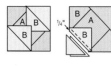

Figure 2

3. Sew a D strip between two C strips with right sides together along the length to make a C-D strip set; press seams toward D. Repeat to make three strip sets.

4. Subcut the C-D strip sets into (38) 3" C-D units as shown in Figure 3.

Figure 3

Romantic Heart
Placement Diagram 60" x 80"

5. To complete one Nine-Patch Square block, sew D to opposite sides of an A-B unit; press seams toward D.

6. Sew a C-D unit to opposite sides of the A-B-D unit to complete one block referring to the block drawing; press seams toward the C-D units.

7. Repeat steps 5 and 6 to make 19 blocks.

Completing the Rose Star Blocks

1. Referring to Figure 4, place an F square on one end of G; stitch on the marked line. Trim seam allowance to ¼"; press F to the right side. Repeat on the opposite end of G, again referring to Figure 4, to complete an F-G unit. Repeat to make 80 F-G units.

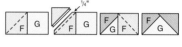

Figure 4

2. To complete one Rose Star block, sew an F-G unit to opposite sides of E to make a center row as shown in Figure 5; press seams toward E.

Figure 5

3. Sew an H square to each end of an F-G unit as shown in Figure 6; press seams toward H. Repeat to make two F-G-H rows.

Figure 6

4. Sew an F-G-H unit to opposite sides of the center row to complete one block as shown in Figure 7; press seams toward the F-G-H rows.

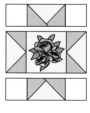

Figure 7

5. Repeat steps 2–4 to make 20 blocks.

Completing the Quilt

1. Join two Rose Star blocks with one Nine-Patch Square block to make an X row as shown in Figure 8; press seams toward the Nine-Patch Square block. Repeat to make three X rows.

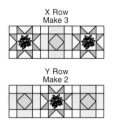

X Row
Make 3

Y Row
Make 2

Figure 8

2. Join two Nine-Patch Square blocks with one Rose Star block to make a Y row, again referring to Figure 8; press seams toward the Nine-Patch Square blocks. Repeat to make two Y rows.

3. Join the rows to complete the pieced center referring to the Placement Diagram; press seams toward the Y rows.

4. Center and sew the I strips to opposite sides of the pieced center, stopping stitching ¼" from each end of the pieced center. Repeat with J strips at the top and bottom.

5. Fold quilt top diagonally with right sides together and align edges as shown in Figure 9; draw a 45-degree-angle line on the top border strip from the end of the border stitching, again referring to Figure 9.

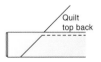

Quilt
top back

Figure 9

6. Stitch along the marked line and trim ¼" from the stitched line as shown in Figure 10; press seam open. Repeat on all corners.

¼"

Figure 10

7. Join three each Rose Star and Nine-Patch Square blocks to make a border strip as shown in Figure 11; press seams toward Nine-Patch Square blocks. Repeat to make four border strips.

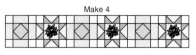

Make 4

Figure 11

8. Sew a border strip to opposite sides of the pieced center, alternating the placement of the strips referring to the Placement Diagram; press seams toward the I strips.

9. Sew the remaining border strips to the top and bottom of the pieced center, alternating the placement of the strips referring to the Placement Diagram; press seams toward the J strips to complete the pieced top.

10. Layer, quilt and bind referring to Finishing Your Quilt on page 176. ■

As the Geese Fly!

Prairie points take on a new use in this pieced
and appliquéd 3-D wall quilt.

DESIGN BY RHONDA TAYLOR

Skill Level: Beginner
Quilt Size: 28" x 28"
Block Size: 6" x 6"
Number of Blocks: 16

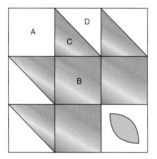

Leaf
6" x 6" Block
Make 8

Geese
6" x 6" Block
Make 8

MATERIALS

- Scrap green tonal
- ⅓ yard coordinating stripe
- ⅜ yard purple tonal
- ¾ yard cream multicolored dot
- ¾ yard blue print
- Backing 34" x 34"
- Batting 34" x 34"
- Neutral-color all-purpose thread
- Quilting thread
- ⅛ yard fusible web
- Basic sewing tools and supplies

Cutting

1. Cut three 2¼" by fabric width coordinating stripe strips for binding.

2. Cut two 4¼" by fabric width purple tonal strips; subcut strips into (16) 4¼" F squares.

3. Cut one 2½" by fabric width cream multicolored dot strip; subcut strip into (16) 2½" A squares.

4. Cut two 2⅞" by fabric width cream multicolored dot strips; subcut strips into (16) 2⅞" squares. Cut each square in half on one diagonal to make 32 D triangles.

5. Cut two 6⅞" by fabric width cream multicolored dot strips; subcut strips into eight 6⅞" squares. Cut each square in half on one diagonal to make 16 E triangles.

6. Cut two 2½" by fabric width blue print strips; subcut strips into (24) 2½" B squares.

7. Cut two 2⅞" by fabric width blue print strips; subcut strips into (16) 2⅞" squares. Cut each square in half on one diagonal to make 32 C triangles.

8. Cut two 2½" x 24½" blue print G strips.

9. Cut two 2½" x 28½" blue print H strips.

Completing the Leaf Blocks

1. Sew C to D along the diagonal to make a C-D unit; repeat to make 32 C-D units.

2. Trace the appliqué leaf shape on page 52 onto the paper side of the fusible web the number of times directed on pattern; cut out shapes leaving a margin around each one.

3. Fuse shapes to the wrong side of green tonal; cut out shapes on traced lines. Remove paper backing.

4. Fold eight of the A squares in half on one diagonal and crease to mark the diagonal center.

5. Center and fuse a leaf shape on the diagonal of each creased A square.

6. To complete one Leaf block, join two C-D units with plain A to make the top row as shown in Figure 1; press seams toward A.

Figure 1

7. Join two B squares with one C-D unit to make the center row as shown in Figure 2; press seams toward outer-edge B.

Figure 2

8. Join one each fused A square, B square and C-D unit to make the bottom row as shown in Figure 3; press seams toward C-D.

Figure 3

9. Join the rows referring to the block drawing to complete one Leaf block; press seams in one direction.

10. Repeat steps 6–9 to complete eight Leaf blocks.

Completing the Geese Blocks

1. Fold each F square in half and in half again to make a prairie point as shown in Figure 4; machine-baste along the raw edge to hold.

Figure 4

2. Pin and baste a folded F 1" from one end on the long side of an E triangle as shown in Figure 5; repeat with all F and E triangles.

Figure 5

3. Join two E-F units along the diagonal to complete one Geese block referring to the block drawing; press seam in one direction.

4. Repeat step 3 to make eight Geese blocks.

Completing the Quilt

1. Join two Leaf blocks with two Geese blocks to make an X row as shown in Figure 6; press seams toward Geese blocks. Repeat to make two X rows.

X Row
Make 2

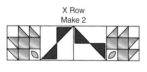

Figure 6

2. Join two Leaf blocks with two Geese blocks to make a Y row as shown in Figure 7; press seams toward Geese blocks. Repeat to make two Y rows.

Y Row
Make 2

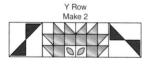

Figure 7

3. Join the X and Y rows referring to the Placement Diagram for positioning of rows; press seams in one direction.

4. Sew a G strip to opposite sides and H strips to the top and bottom of the pieced center; press seams toward G and H strips.

5. Layer, quilt and bind referring to Finishing Your Quilt on page 176. **Note:** *The sample used hand-quilting stitches to hold the fused leaf shapes in place.* ■

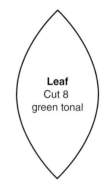

Leaf
Cut 8
green tonal

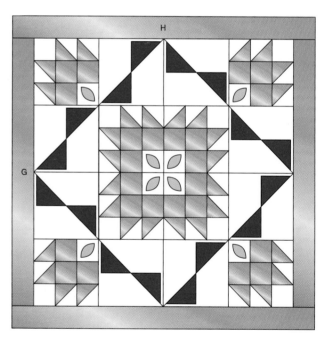

As the Geese Fly!
Placement Diagram 28" x 28"

Nine-Patch Twirl

Dazzle your friends with magic. This cute quilt has what is known as a Disappearing Nine-Patch block. Can you find the Nine-Patch?

DESIGN BY CAROLYN S. VAGTS FOR THE VILLAGE PATTERN COMPANY

PROJECT SPECIFICATIONS

Skill Level: Beginner
Quilt Size: 40½" x 53½"
Block Size: 11½" x 11½"
Number of Blocks: 12

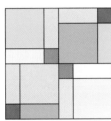

Nine-Patch Twirl
11½" x 11½" Block
Make 12

MATERIALS

- 27 fat eighths (9" x 21") assorted bright colors
- ¾ yard white tonal
- Backing 47" x 60"
- Batting 47" x 60"
- Neutral-color all-purpose thread
- Quilting thread
- Basic sewing tools and supplies

Cutting

1. Cut one 4½" by fabric width strip from each fat eighth; subcut each strip into four 4½" squares to cut a total of 108 A squares.

2. Cut one 2½" by fabric width strip from 10 fat eighths for binding.

3. Cut (11) 2" by fabric width white tonal strips. Subcut three strips into eight 2" x 12" B strips. Cut five strips into five 2" x 38" C strips. Set aside three strips for D.

Completing the Blocks

1. Select nine different A squares. Stitch into three rows of three A squares referring to Figure 1. Press seams in opposite directions.

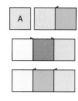

Figure 1

2. Stitch the A square rows into a Nine-Batch unit referring again to Figure 1; press seams in one direction.

3. Repeat steps 1 and 2 to make a total of 12 Nine-Patch units.

4. Rotary-cut the units in half horizontally and vertically to make four 6¼"-square quarter units per Nine-Patch unit as shown in Figure 2.

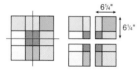

Figure 2

5. To complete one block, select four quarter units from different Nine-Patch units. Arrange the quarter units, turning them to make a Nine-Patch Twirl block referring to the block drawing and the Placement Diagram for positioning. Stitch quarter units together as arranged to make a 12"-square block. Repeat to make 12 blocks.

Completing the Quilt

1. Stitch two B strips between three blocks to make a row as shown in Figure 3. Press seams toward B. Repeat to make a total of 4 rows.

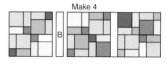

Figure 3

2. Stitch rows together with five C strips beginning and ending with a C strip and referring to the Placement Diagram. Press seams toward C.

3. Stitch D strips together on short ends; press seams open. Subcut strip into two 2" x 54"-long D strips.

4. Stitch a D strip on each long side of the quilt top.

5. Layer, quilt and bind referring to Finishing Your Quilt on page 176. ■

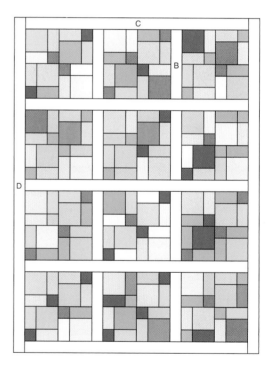

Nine-Patch Twirl
Placement Diagram 40½" x 53½"

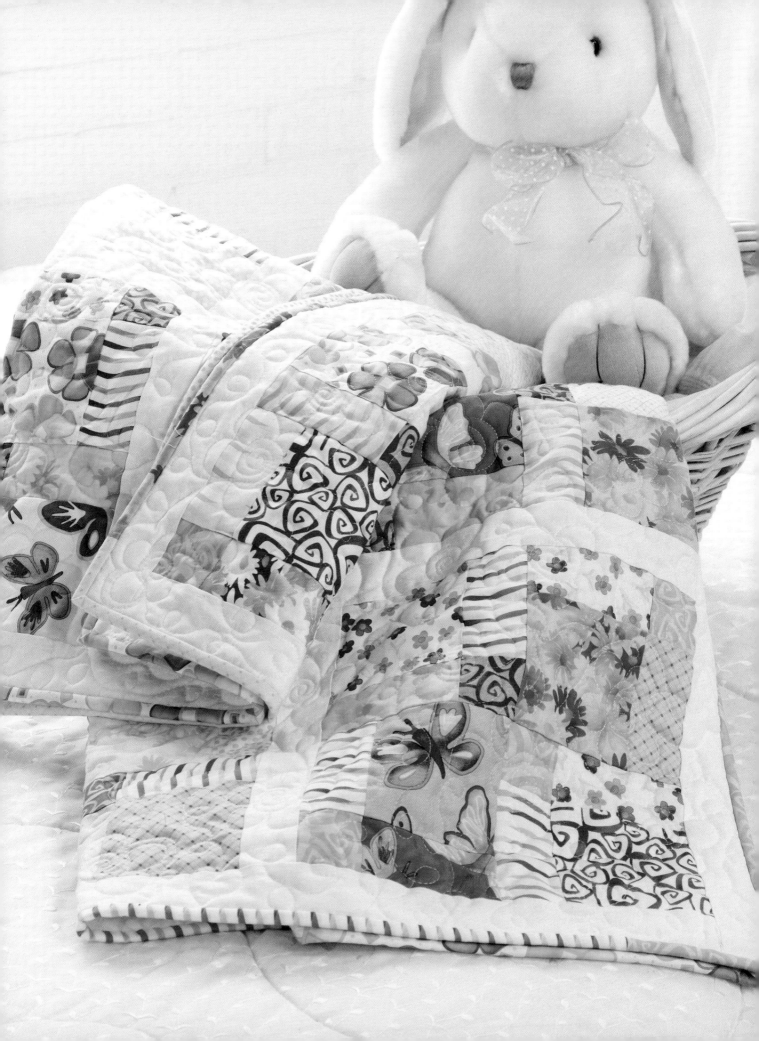

Beach Buddy

Stitch up some blocks and machine-quilt them onto a large
beach towel to show off your talent on your next trip to the beach.

DESIGN BY DEBORAH A. HOBBS FOR TA DAH

PROJECT SPECIFICATIONS

Skill Level: Beginner
Quilt Size: 42" x 63" (patchwork only)
Block Size: 10½" x 10½"
Number of Blocks: 24

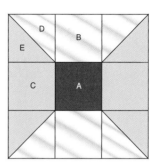

Beach Buddy
10½" x 10½" Block
Make 24

MATERIALS

- ½ yard red/orange houndstooth print
- 1½ yards white floral
- 1½ yards cream/peach print
- All-purpose thread to match
- Quilting thread
- Large beach towel at least 42" x 63"
- Basic sewing tools and supplies

Cutting

1. Cut three 4" by fabric width red/orange houndstooth print strips; subcut into (24) 4" A squares.

2. Cut five 4" by fabric width white floral strips; subcut strips into (48) 4" B squares.

3. Cut six 4⅜" by fabric width white floral strips; subcut strips into (48) 4⅜" squares. Cut each square in half on one diagonal to make 96 D triangles.

4. Cut five 4" by fabric width cream/peach print strips; subcut strips into (48) 4" C squares.

5. Cut six 4⅜" by fabric width cream/peach print strips; subcut strips into (48) 4⅜" squares. Cut each square in half on one diagonal to make 96 E triangles.

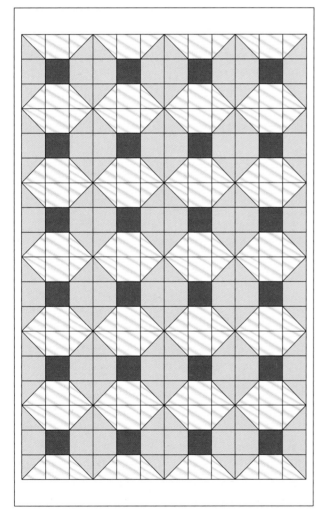

Beach Buddy
Placement Diagram 42" x 63" (patchwork only)

Completing the Blocks

1. Sew D to E along the diagonal to make a D-E unit as shown in Figure 1; press seam toward E. Repeat to make 96 D-E units.

Make 96

Figure 1

2. To complete one Beach Buddy block, sew a C square to opposite sides of A; press seams toward C.

3. Sew a D-E unit to opposite sides of B as shown in Figure 2 to make the top row; press seams toward B. Repeat to make the bottom row.

Figure 2

4. Sew the A-C row between the top and bottom rows referring to the block drawing to complete one Beach Buddy block.

5. Repeat steps 2–4 to complete 24 Beach Buddy blocks.

Completing the Quilt

1. Join four Beach Buddy blocks to make a row referring to Figure 3; press seams in one direction. Repeat to make six rows.

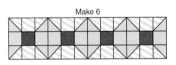

Make 6

Figure 3

2. Join the rows to complete the patchwork section.

3. Center the patchwork section on the beach towel; fold edges of patchwork section under as necessary to leave an even margin on each side and at the top and bottom. Baste to hold in place. ***Note:*** *On the sample shown, the patchwork section was folded under 2" on each side and ¼" on the top and bottom, leaving a 1" margin on long sides and 3½" on the top and bottom of the towel.*

4. Machine-quilt as desired to hold the layers together; machine-stitch close to folded edges all around to secure patchwork to towel. ◼

Weathervane Stars

Dewy blues and blushing pinks make a perfect color combination for early summer. Traditionally set blocks and needle-turn appliqué are highlighted in this gem of a quilt.

DESIGN BY NORMA STORM

PROJECT SPECIFICATIONS

Skill Level: Intermediate
Finished Size: 24" x 24"
Block Size: 6" x 6"
Number of Blocks: 9

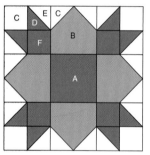

Weathervane Star
6" x 6" Block
Make 5

Square Corners
6" x 6" Block
Make 4

MATERIALS

- Scrap yellow tonal
- ⅛ yard green batik
- ⅛ yard pink batik
- ⅜ yard blue butterfly batik
- ½ yard blue tonal
- ⅔ yard white tonal
- Backing 30" x 30"
- Batting 30" x 30"
- All-purpose thread to match fabrics
- Quilting thread
- Scrap polyester fiberfill
- Template material
- Water-soluble marker or pencil
- Basic sewing tools and supplies

Cutting

1. Prepare templates for hand appliqué using patterns given. Trace shapes onto the right side of fabrics using a water-soluble marker or pencil as directed on patterns for color; cut out shapes adding a ⅛"–¼" seam allowance all around for hand appliqué.

2. Turn seam allowance to the wrong side along marked lines; baste to hold. Remove marks. **Note:** *Do not turn under seam allowance on edges that will be covered with another piece.*

3. Cut four 2½" by fabric width blue butterfly batik strips. Subcut strips into (20) 2½" B squares and (32) 2½" H squares.

4. Cut one 2½" by fabric width blue tonal strip; subcut strip into five 2½" A squares.

5. Cut one 1½" by fabric width blue tonal strip; subcut strip into (20) 1½" F squares.

6. Cut one 1⅞" by fabric width blue tonal strip; subcut strip into (20) 1⅞" D squares. Cut each square in half on one diagonal to make 40 D triangles.

7. Cut three 2¼" by fabric width blue tonal strips for binding.

8. Cut three 1½" by fabric width white tonal strips; subcut strips into (60) 1½" C squares.

9. Cut two 6½" by fabric width white tonal strips. Subcut strips into four 6½" G squares, (12) 3½" x 6½" I rectangles and four 3½" K squares.

10. Cut one 1⅞" by fabric width white tonal strip; subcut strip into (20) 1⅞" E squares. Cut each square in half on one diagonal to make 40 E triangles.

Completing the Weathervane Star Blocks

1. Mark a diagonal line from corner to corner on the wrong side of 40 C squares.

2. Place a marked C square right sides together on one corner of B and stitch on the marked line as shown in Figure 1; trim seam to ¼" and press C to the right side, again referring to Figure 1.

Figure 1

3. Repeat step 2 on the adjacent corner of B as shown in Figure 2 to complete a B-C unit. Repeat to make 20 B-C units.

Figure 2

4. Sew D to E along the diagonal to make a D-E unit; press seam toward D. Repeat to make 40 D-E units.

5. Sew one D-E unit to C to make a C-D-E unit as shown in Figure 3; press seam toward C. Repeat with D-E and F, again referring to Figure 3; press seam toward F.

Figure 3

6. Join the D-E-F unit with the C-D-E unit to complete a corner unit, again referring to Figure 3.

7. Repeat steps 5 and 6 to complete 20 corner units.

8. To complete one Weathervane Star block, sew a B-C unit to opposite sides of A to make the center row as shown in Figure 4; press seams toward A.

Figure 4

9. Sew a corner unit to opposite sides of a B-C unit to make a top and bottom row referring to Figure 5; press seams toward corner units.

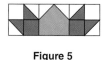

Figure 5

10. Sew the center row between the top and bottom rows referring to the block drawing for positioning to complete one Weathervane Star block; press seams toward the center row.

11. Repeat steps 8–10 to complete five Weathervane Star blocks.

Completing the Square Corners Blocks

1. Mark a diagonal line on the wrong side of all H squares.

2. Place an H square right sides together on each corner of G and stitch on the marked lines as shown in Figure 6; trim seams to ¼" and press H to the right side to complete one Square Corners block.

Figure 6

3. Repeat step 2 to complete four Square Corners blocks.

Completing the Quilt

1. Sew H to two corners of I as in step 2 of Completing the Square Corners Blocks to complete an H-I unit as shown in Figure 7; repeat to make eight H-I units.

Figure 7

2. Join one I rectangle with two K squares and two H-I units to complete an X row as shown in Figure 8; press seams toward H-I units. Repeat to make two X rows.

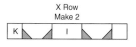

Figure 8

3. Join one Square Corners block with two Weathervane Star blocks and two H-I units to complete a Y row as shown in Figure 9; press seams away from Weathervane Star blocks. Repeat to make two Y rows.

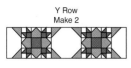

Y Row
Make 2

Figure 9

4. Join one Weathervane Star block with two Square Corners blocks and two I rectangles to complete a Z row as shown in Figure 10; press seams away from the Weathervane Star block.

Z Row
Make 1

Figure 10

5. Referring to the Placement Diagram, arrange and join the X, Y and Z rows to complete the pieced top; press seams in one direction.

6. Arrange flower and leaf motifs in the white background areas of the pieced top referring to the Placement Diagram for suggested positioning; hand-stitch motifs in place using thread to match fabrics, stuffing a tiny bit of fiberfill behind each yellow flower center before final stitching to complete the quilt top.

7. Layer, quilt and bind referring to Finishing Your Quilt on page 176. ◼

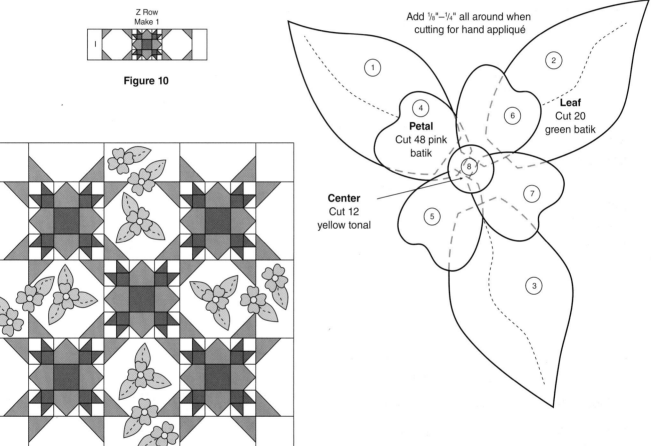

Add ⅛"–¼" all around when cutting for hand appliqué

Leaf
Cut 20
green batik

Petal
Cut 48 pink
batik

Center
Cut 12
yellow tonal

Weathervane Stars
Placement Diagram 24" x 24"

Dressed to the Nines

Make your home a showplace. These quilts dress up any room, bed or sofa when you add your fabrics to the designs.

Stars Squared

Two blocks combine to form stars in this colorful bed-size quilt.

DESIGN BY LUCY FAZELY & MICHAEL L. BURNS

PROJECT SPECIFICATIONS

Skill Level: Advanced
Quilt Size: 73" x 86½"
Block Size: 13½" x 13½"
Number of Blocks: 20

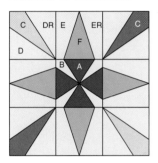

Blue Star
13½" x 13½" Block
Make 10

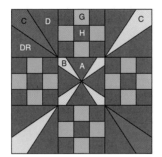

Nine-Patch Star
13½" x 13½" Block
Make 10

MATERIALS

- ⅓ yard pink dot
- ⅜ yard blue plaid
- ¾ yard purple dot
- 1¼ yards blue tonal
- 1⅓ yards lavender dot
- 1½ yards pale blue tonal
- 1¾ yards black print
- 2⅛ yards black swirl print
- Backing 79" x 93"
- Batting 79" x 93"
- Neutral-color all-purpose thread
- Quilting thread
- Template material
- Basic sewing tools and supplies

Cutting

1. Cut two 3⅞" by fabric width pink dot B strips.

2. Cut three 2¾" by fabric width blue plaid A strips.

3. Cut three 7" by fabric width purple dot C strips.

4. Cut from blue tonal: two 5" by fabric width F strips, eight 2" by fabric width G strips and seven 1½" by fabric width K/L strips.

5. Cut three 7" by fabric width C strips and seven 3" by fabric width O/P strips from lavender dot.

6. Cut from pale blue tonal: two 3⅞" by fabric width B strips, four 5" by fabric width D/DR strips and four 5" by fabric width E/ER strips.

7. Cut eight 4½" by fabric width black print Q/R strips and eight 2¼" by fabric width black print strips for binding.

8. Cut from black swirl print: three 2¾" by fabric width A strips, four 5" by fabric width D/DR strips, (10) 2" by fabric width H strips and (13) 1½" by fabric width I/J/M/N strips.

9. Prepare templates A, B, C, D/DR, E/ER and F using patterns on page 67.

10. Refer to Figure 1 for template layout and cut pieces from strips as directed on patterns.

Figure 1

Completing the Blue Star Blocks

1. To complete one Blue Star block, stitch a pale blue B to a blue plaid A to make an A-B unit as shown in Figure 2; press seam toward B. Repeat to make four A-B units.

Make 4

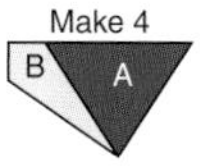

Figure 2    **Figure 3**

2. Join two A-B units as shown in Figure 3; press seam toward B. Repeat. Join the two pieced units to complete the center unit, again referring to Figure 3; press seam in one direction.

3. Stitch a pale blue D and DR to a lavender C as shown in Figure 4; press seams toward D and DR. Repeat to make two lavender C-D units.

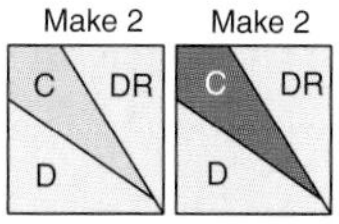

Figure 4

4. Repeat step 3 with pale blue D and DR, and purple C to make two purple C-D units again referring to Figure 4.

5. Stitch E and ER to a blue F to complete an E-F unit as shown in Figure 5; press seams toward E and ER. Repeat to make four E-F units.

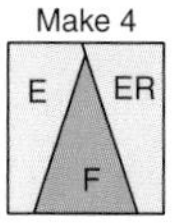

Figure 5   **Figure 6**

6. Stitch an E-F unit to opposite sides of the center unit to complete the center row as shown in Figure 6; press seams toward the center unit.

7. Stitch a lavender C-D unit to one side and a purple C-D unit to the opposite side of an E-F unit to complete the top row as shown in Figure 7; press seams away from E-F. Repeat to make the bottom row.

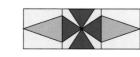

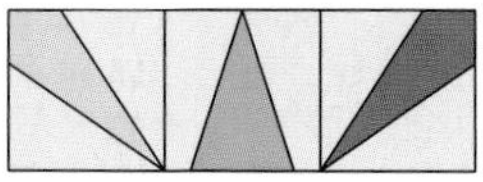

Figure 7

8. Stitch the center row between the top and bottom rows referring to the block drawing to complete one Blue Star block; press seams away from the center row.

9. Repeat steps 1–8 to complete 10 Blue Star blocks.

Completing the Nine-Patch Star Blocks

1. Stitch an H strip between two G strips along length; press seams toward H. Repeat to make two G-H-G strip sets.

2. Subcut the G-H-G strip sets into (40) 2" G-H-G units as shown in Figure 8.

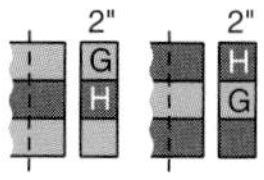

Figure 8

3. Stitch a G strip between two H strips along length; press seams toward H. Repeat to make four H-G-H strip sets.

4. Subcut the H-G-H strip sets into (80) 2" H-G-H units, again referring to Figure 8.

5. Stitch a G-H-G unit between two H-G-H units to complete a G-H unit referring to Figure 9; press seams in one direction. Repeat to make 40 G-H units.

Make 40

Figure 9

6. To complete one Nine-Patch Star block, stitch a pink B to a black swirl A as shown in Figure 10; press seams toward B. Repeat to make four A-B units.

Make 4

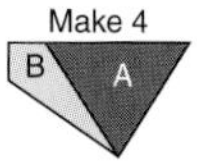

Figure 10

7. Join two A-B units as shown in Figure 11; press seam toward B. Repeat. Join the two pieced units to complete the center unit, again referring to Figure 11; press seam in one direction.

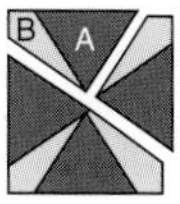

Figure 11

8. Stitch a lavender C between a black swirl D and DR to make a lavender/black C-D unit as shown in Figure 12; press seams toward C.

Figure 12

9. Repeat step 8 with black swirl D and DR, and purple C to make two purple/black C-D units again referring to Figure 12.

10. Stitch the center unit between two G-H units to make the center row as shown in Figure 13; press seams toward the G-H units.

Figure 13

11. Stitch a G-H unit between one each purple/black and lavender/black C-D unit to make the top row as shown in Figure 14; press seams toward the G-H unit. Repeat to make the bottom row.

Figure 14

12. Stitch the center row between the top and bottom rows to complete the Nine-Patch Star block referring to the block drawing for positioning; press seams toward the center row.

13. Repeat steps 6–12 to complete 10 Nine-Patch Star blocks.

Completing the Quilt

1. Join two Blue Star blocks with two Nine-Patch Star blocks to make a block row, alternating blocks; press seams toward the Nine-Patch Star blocks. Repeat to make five rows.

2. Join the rows referring to the Placement Diagram for positioning; press seams in one direction to complete the pieced center.

3. Join the I/J/M/N strips on short ends to make one long strip; press seams open. Subcut strip into two strips each of the following sizes: 1½" x 68" I, 1½" x 56½" J, 1½" x 72" M and 1½" x 60½" N.

4. Repeat step 3 with K/L strips; subcut two strips each 1½" x 70" K and 1½" x 58½" L.

5. Stitch I strips to opposite long sides and J strips to the top and bottom of the pieced center; press seams toward I and J strips.

6. Repeat step 5 with K, L, M and N strips in alphabetical order on the sides first and then top and bottom; press seams toward most recently added strips.

7. Repeat step 3 with the O/P strips; subcut two strips each 3" x 74" O and 3" x 65½" P.

8. Stitch O strips to opposite long sides and P strips to the top and bottom of the pieced center; press seams toward O and P strips.

9. Repeat step 3 with Q/R strips; subcut two strips each 4½" x 79" Q and 4½" x 73½" R.

10. Stitch the Q strips to opposite long sides and R strips to the top and bottom to complete the pieced top; press seams toward Q and R strips.

11. Layer, quilt and bind referring to Finishing Your Quilt on page 176. ■

Stars Squared
Placement Diagram 73" x 86½"

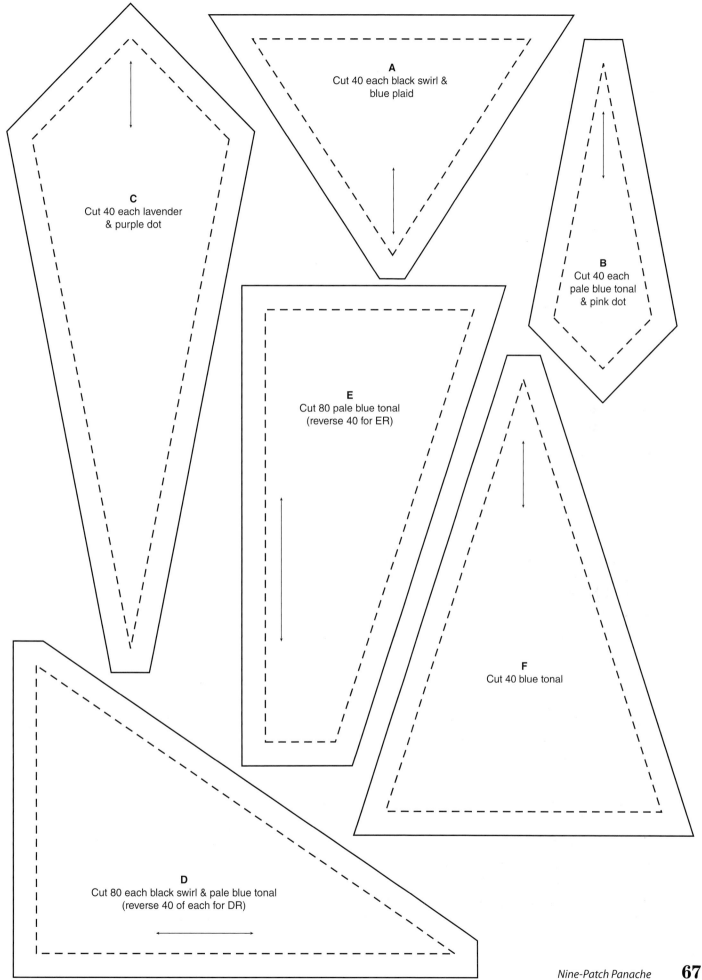

A
Cut 40 each black swirl &
blue plaid

B
Cut 40 each
pale blue tonal
& pink dot

C
Cut 40 each lavender
& purple dot

E
Cut 80 pale blue tonal
(reverse 40 for ER)

F
Cut 40 blue tonal

D
Cut 80 each black swirl & pale blue tonal
(reverse 40 of each for DR)

Royal Cherries

Add a retro wall quilt to your dining area or maybe a foyer. Choose the fabrics for you and set the pace. It can be whatever you want it to be.

DESIGN BY SUSAN GETMAN

PROJECT SPECIFICATIONS

Skill Level: Confident Beginner
Wall Quilt Size: 32" x 44"
Block Sizes: 6" x 6", 3¾" x 3¾"
Number of Blocks: 15 and 30

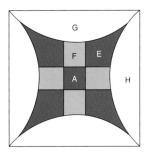

Curved Nine-Patch
6" x 6" Block
Make 8

Cherries
6" x 6" Block
Make 7

Nine-Patch Tan
3¾" x 3¾" Block
Make 15

Nine-Patch Cream
3¾" x 3¾" Block
Make 15

PROJECT NOTE

To make this wall quilt with dark red fabric scraps, make cutting templates for E (2⅞" x 2⅞") and A (1¾" x 1¾"). Trace the templates and cut the total number of pieces listed from a wide variety of dark red fabrics. The more you use, the more interesting the quilt will be.

MATERIALS

- Scraps assorted dark green tonals
- ⅞ yard light tan print
- ⅝ yard cream print
- 1½ yards total assorted dark red prints
- Backing 40" x 52"
- Batting 40" x 52"
- Neutral-color all-purpose thread
- Coordinating appliqué thread
- Quilting thread
- 1 yard paper-backed fusible web
- 1 yard fabric stabilizer
- Basic sewing tools and supplies

Cutting

1. Cut four 1¾" by fabric width light tan print strips; subcut strips into (75) 1¾" C squares.

2. Cut two 6½" by fabric width light tan print strips; subcut strips into (7) 6½" D squares.

3. Cut two 2⅞" by fabric width light tan print strips; subcut strips into (32) 1¾" x 2⅞" F rectangles.

4. Cut three 1¾" by fabric width cream print strips; subcut strips into (60) 1¾" B squares.

5. Cut three 2⅞" by fabric width dark red print strips; subcut strips into (32) 2⅞" E squares.

6. Cut seven 1¾" by fabric width dark red print strips; subcut strips into (143) 1¾" A squares.

7. Cut eight 2¼" by fabric width dark red print strips. Set aside four strips for binding and four strips for K/L.

8. Cut three 2" by fabric width dark red print I/J strips.

9. Referring to patterns for number of pieces needed, trace cherries motif appliqué shapes and G onto the paper side of fusible web leaving ½" between shapes. Cut out shapes leaving ¼" margin on each piece.

10. Following manufacturer's instructions, fuse cutout shapes to the wrong side of dark green tonal scraps, and remaining cream and dark red print fabrics as instructed on patterns. Cut around each shape on the traced lines.

Completing the Nine-Patch Blocks

1. To complete one block, select four A and five C squares. Stitch an A between two C squares to make a top row as shown in Figure 1. Press seams to the right. Repeat to make a bottom row.

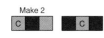

Make 2

Figure 1

2. Stitch a C between two A squares to make a center row, again referring to Figure 1; press seams to the left.

3. Stitch the center row between the top and bottom rows, matching seams to make a Nine-Patch Tan block referring to the block drawing. Press seams in one direction.

4. Repeat steps 1–3 to make 15 Nine-Patch Tan blocks.

5. Repeat steps 1–3 to make 15 Nine-Patch Cream blocks using four B squares and five A squares for each block and referring to the block drawing.

Completing the Curved Nine-Patch Blocks

1. To complete one block, select four each E squares and F rectangles, one A square and four G appliqué shapes. Stitch F between two E rectangles to make a top row as shown in Figure 2. Press seams to the right. Repeat to make a bottom row.

Make 2

Figure 2

2. Stitch A between two F rectangles to make a center row, again referring to Figure 2; press seams to the left.

3. Stitch the center row between the top and bottom rows matching seams to make a Nine-Patch unit as shown in Figure 3. Press seams in one direction.

Figure 3

4. Remove the paper backing from one G appliqué shape and position G on the left side of the Nine-Patch unit as shown in Figure 4; fuse in place. Repeat on right side of unit, again referring to Figure 4.

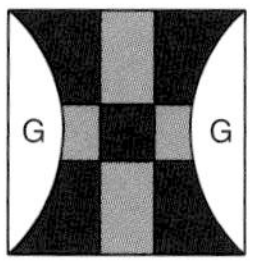

Figure 4

5. Position and fuse a G shape to the top and the bottom of the Nine-Patch unit as shown in Figure 5.

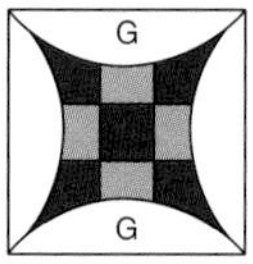

Figure 5

6. Stitch the curved edges of G appliqué shapes using a short, narrow blanket stitch and invisible or matching thread.

7. Repeat steps 1–6 to make eight Curved Nine-Patch blocks.

Completing the Cherries Blocks

1. Fold and crease each D square to mark center.

2. To complete one block, arrange and fuse the cherries motif appliqué pieces on the center of a D square referring to the appliqué motif and Cherries block drawing. Repeat to make seven blocks.

3. Pin a square of fabric stabilizer to the back of each block. Use matching or invisible thread to machine-stitch a short, narrow blanket stitch around the appliqué pieces. Carefully remove stabilizer. Repeat on all Cherries blocks.

Completing the Quilt

1. Stitch a Cherries block between two Curved Nine-Patch blocks to make an X row as shown in Figure 6; press seams toward the Cherries block. Repeat to make three X rows.

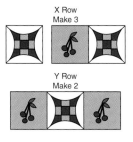

Figure 6

2. Stitch a Curved Nine-Patch block between two Cherries blocks to make a Y row, again referring to Figure 6; press seams toward the Cherries blocks. Repeat to make two Y rows.

3. Stitch rows together alternately beginning with an X row and referring to the Placement Diagram to complete the pieced center. Press seams in one direction.

4. Stitch I/J strips together on the short ends; press seams open. Subcut strip into two 2" x 30½" I inner borders and two 2" x 21½" J inner borders.

5. Stitch I borders to opposite long sides of the pieced center and J to the top and bottom referring to the Placement Diagram; press seams toward I and J.

6. Select four each Nine-Patch Tan and Nine-Patch Cream blocks. Stitch together alternately beginning with a Nine-Patch Tan block referring to Figure 7. Repeat to make two pieced A borders.

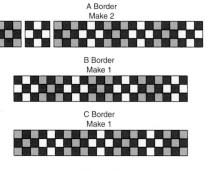

Figure 7

7. Select three Nine-Patch Tan and four Nine-Patch Cream blocks and stitch together beginning with a Nine-Patch Cream block, again referring to Figure 7, to make one pieced B border.

8. Select four Nine-Patch Tan and three Nine-Patch Cream blocks and sew together beginning with a Nine-Patch Tan block, again referring to Figure 7, to make one pieced C border.

9. Stitch A borders to opposite sides of the pieced center as shown in Figure 8; press seams toward I. Stitch B border to the top and C border to the bottom of the pieced center, again referring to Figure 8; press seams toward J.

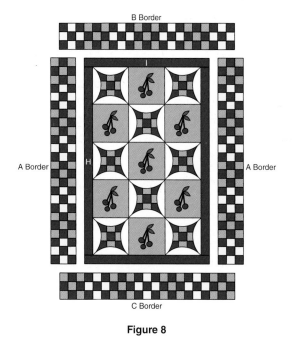

Figure 8

10. Stitch K/L strips together on the short ends and press seams open. Cut two 2¼" x 41" K outer borders and two 2¼" x 32½" L outer borders.

11. Stitch K borders to opposite long sides of the pieced center and L to the top and bottom referring to the Placement Diagram; press seams toward K and L.

12. Layer, quilt and bind referring to Finishing Your Quilt on page 176. ∎

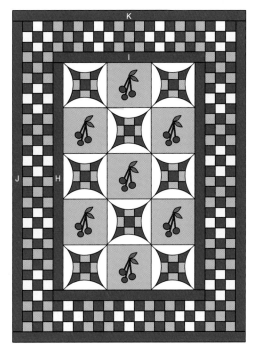

Royal Cherries
Placement Diagram 32" x 44"

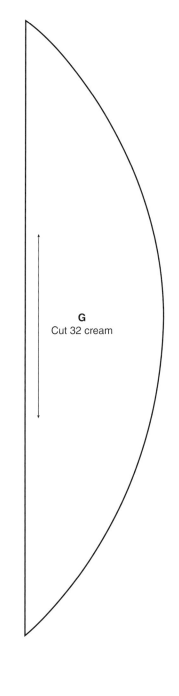

G
Cut 32 cream

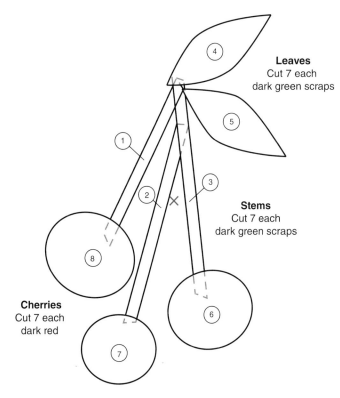

Leaves
Cut 7 each
dark green scraps

Stems
Cut 7 each
dark green scraps

Cherries
Cut 7 each
dark red

Dots & Prints

Darks and lights create contrast in the blocks of this simple quilt.

DESIGN BY MICHELE CRAWFORD

PROJECT SPECIFICATIONS

Skill Level: Beginner
Quilt Size: 59" x 71"
Block Size: 12" x 12"
Number of Blocks: 20

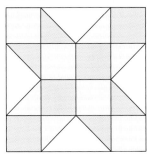

Dots & Prints
12" x 12" Block
Make 20

MATERIALS

- ⅝ yard each yellow, gray and olive prints
- ⅝ yard each yellow, gray, olive and blue dots
- 1 yard navy print
- 1⅞ yards white solid
- Backing 65" x 77"
- Batting 65" x 77"
- All-purpose thread to match fabrics
- Quilting thread
- Basic sewing tools and supplies

Cutting

1. Cut four 3½" by fabric width strips each dot and print fabric. Subcut strips of each color into 40 each 3½" A (dot) and B (print) squares.

2. Cut seven 6½" by fabric width strips white solid; subcut strips into (80) 3½" x 6½" C rectangles.

3. Cut six 1½" by fabric width strips white solid. Join strips on short ends to make one long strip; subcut strip into two 1½" x 48½" D strips and two 1½" x 62½" E strips.

4. Cut four 5" G squares white solid.

5. Cut two 2½" by fabric width strips each dot and print fabric for F borders.

6. Cut seven 2¼" by fabric width strips navy print for binding.

Piecing the Blocks

1. To make one same-color block, join two A and two B squares to make a Four-Patch center; press seams toward B.

2. Draw a line from corner to corner on the wrong side of four each A and B squares.

3. Referring to Figure 1, place A on one end of C and stitch on the marked line. Trim seam to ¼"; press A to the right side.

Figure 1

4. Repeat step 3 with B on the opposite end of C, again referring to Figure 1. Repeat to make two A-B-C units.

5. Repeat steps 3 and 4 to make two reversed A-B-C side units referring to Figure 2.

Figure 2

Figure 3

6. Sew a side unit to opposite sides of the Four-Patch center to make center unit as shown in Figure 3; press seams toward the Four-Patch center.

7. Sew an A square to the B end and a B square to the A end of an A-B-C unit as shown in Figure 4; repeat for two top/bottom units.

Make 2

Figure 4

8. Sew a top/bottom unit to the remaining sides of the center unit to complete one block; press seams toward the newly added units.

9. Repeat steps 1–8 to complete five each yellow, gray, olive and navy blocks.

Completing the Top

1. Arrange the blocks in five rows of four blocks each referring to the Placement Diagram for positioning of blocks. **Note:** *Blocks of the same color form diagonal lines across the quilt top.*

2. Join blocks in rows; press seams in one direction, pressing adjacent rows in opposite directions. Join rows to complete the pieced center; press seams in one direction.

3. Sew D to the top and bottom, and E to opposite long sides of the pieced center; press seams toward strips.

4. Join one F strip each print and then dot in the following color order as shown in Figure 5: gray, yellow, olive and navy/blue; press seams in one direction. Repeat for two strip sets.

Figure 5

5. Subcut strip sets into (14) 5" F segments, again referring to Figure 5.

6. Join four segments starting with gray print and continue in the same order to make one strip. Repeat for two side strips.

7. Repeat step 6 with three segments to make two top/bottom strips.

8. Remove a gray print piece from the beginning end of each side strip and sew one to the blue dot end of each top/bottom strip as shown in Figure 6.

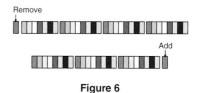

Figure 6

9. Sew a side strip to opposite long sides of the pieced center referring to the Placement Diagram for positioning of strips; press seams toward E.

10. Sew a G square to each end of each top/bottom strip; press seams toward G. Sew a strip to the top and bottom of the pieced center referring to the Placement Diagram for positioning of strips; press seams toward D to complete the top.

11. Layer, quilt and bind referring to Finishing Your Quilt on page 176. ▥

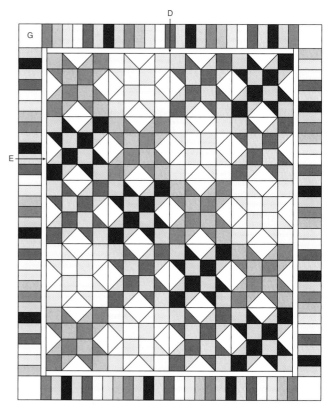

Dots & Prints
Placement Diagram 59" x 71"

An Autumn Evening

Fiery orange stars shine brightly on the black background of this beautiful quilt.

DESIGN BY TOBY LISCHKO

PROJECT SPECIFICATIONS

Skill Level: Intermediate
Quilt Size: 85" x 102"
Block Size: 12" x 12"
Number of Blocks: 32

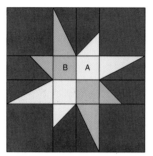

Autumn Evening
12" x 12" Block
Make 32

MATERIALS

- ⅝ yard orange/gold tonal
- ¾ yard orange tonal
- 1¼ yards total orange tonals
- 1⅓ yards total yellow/gold tonals
- 7½ yards black tonal
- Backing 91" x 108"
- Batting 91" x 108"
- Neutral-color all-purpose thread
- Quilting thread
- Basic sewing tools and supplies

PROJECT NOTES

The quilt shown uses a variety of orange and yellow tonals to create the blocks. If you choose to use scraps or a variety of fabrics, be sure to use the same fabrics in the outside points as the Four-Patch centers. When creating the Four-Patch centers using a variety of fabrics, cut fabric-width strips as directed to total length needed as instructed in the cutting instructions.

Cutting

1. Cut eight 2" by fabric width strips orange/gold tonal for borders. Join strips on short ends to make one long strip; press seams open. Subcut strip into two 2" x 90" K strips and two 2" x 73" L strips.

2. Cut (10) 2¼" by fabric width strips orange tonal for binding.

3. Cut four 2½" by fabric width strips each yellow/gold (A) and orange (B) tonals.

4. Cut three strips each 4½" by fabric width orange (C) and yellow/gold (CC) tonals and five strips black tonal (D). Prepare template for C/CC/D using pattern given; cut 64 each C and CC, and 128 D pieces from the strips using the template as shown in Figure 1.

Figure 1

5. Cut four 2½" by fabric width strips each yellow/gold (F) and orange (G) tonals; subcut strips into 64 each 2½" F and G squares.

6. Cut (15) 4½" by fabric width strips black tonal; subcut strips into (128) 4½" H squares.

7. Cut four 18¼" squares black tonal; cut each square in half on both diagonals to make 16 I triangles. Set aside two triangles for another project.

8. Cut two 9⅜" squares black tonal; cut each square in half on one diagonal to make four J triangles.

9. Cut eight 4½" by fabric width strips black tonal; subcut strips into (128) 2½" x 4½" E rectangles.

10. Cut (10) 7½" by fabric width strips black tonal. Join strips on short ends to make one long strip; press seams open. Subcut strip into two 7½" x 106" M strips and two 7½" x 90" N strips.

Completing the Blocks

Note: *Use one orange tonal and one yellow/gold tonal per block.*

1. Stitch an A strip to a B strip with right sides together along length; press seam in one direction. Repeat for four strip sets. Subcut strip sets into (64) 2½" A-B segments as shown in Figure 2.

Figure 2

2. Join two A-B segments to make an A-B unit as shown in Figure 3; press seams in one direction. Repeat for 32 A-B units.

Figure 3

3. Sew C to D as shown in Figure 4; repeat to make 64 C-D units. Press seams toward D. Repeat to make 64 CC-D units, again referring to Figure 4.

Figure 4

4. Mark a line from corner to corner on the wrong side of all F and G squares.

5. Place an F square on one end of E as shown in Figure 5; stitch on the marked line, trim seam to ¼" and press F to the right side, again referring to Figure 5. Repeat to make 64 each E-F and E-G units as shown in Figure 6.

Figure 5   **Figure 6**

6. To complete one block, join a C-D unit with an E-F unit as shown in Figure 7; repeat for two units. Press seams toward E-F. Repeat with CC-D and E-G to make two units, again referring to Figure 7.

Figure 7

7. Arrange and join the pieced units in rows with an A-B unit and four H squares as shown in Figure 8. Press seams toward A-B and H.

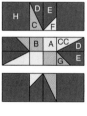

Figure 8

8. Join the rows to complete one block; press seams in one direction.

9. Repeat steps 6–8 to make 32 blocks.

Completing the Top

1. Arrange and join the blocks in diagonal rows with the I and J triangles referring to Figure 9. Press seams in adjacent rows in opposite directions.

Figure 9

2. Join the rows to complete the quilt center; press seams in one direction.

3. Center and stitch a K strip to opposite long sides and L strips to the top and bottom, mitering corners; trim mitered seams to ¼" and press seams open as shown in Figure 10.

Figure 10

4. Center and stitch an M strip to opposite long sides and N strips to the top and bottom, mitering corners; trim mitered seams to ¼" and press seams open as in step 3.

5. Layer, quilt and bind referring to Finishing Your Quilt on page 176. ■

An Autumn Evening
Placement Diagram 85" x 102"

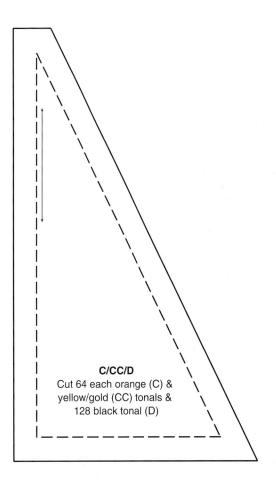

C/CC/D
Cut 64 each orange (C) & yellow/gold (CC) tonals & 128 black tonal (D)

Spring Fling

Bright and cheery flannels create a warm quilt for those cold nights in early spring.

DESIGN BY KARLA SCHULZ

PROJECT SPECIFICATIONS

Skill Level: Beginner
Quilt Size: 76½" x 102"
Block Size: 18" x 18"
Number of Blocks: 14

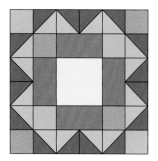

Spring Fling
18" x 18" Block
Make 14

MATERIALS

All fabrics are flannel tonals
- ⅝ yard each aqua and pink
- 1⅛ yards purple
- 1½ yards green
- 2¼ yards yellow
- 4⅜ yards blue
- Backing 83" x 108"
- Batting 83" x 108"
- Neutral-color all-purpose thread
- Hand- or machine-quilting thread
- Rotary ruler with 45-degree-angle line
- Basic sewing tools and supplies

Cutting

1. Cut three 6½" by fabric width strips yellow; subcut strips into (14) 6½" A squares.

2. Cut six 5" by fabric width strips yellow; subcut strips into four 5" x 18" I and four 5" x 23" J rectangles. Set aside remaining two strips to make G units.

3. Cut five 6½" by fabric width strips purple; subcut strips into (56) 3½" x 6½" B rectangles.

4. Cut five 3½" by fabric width strips each pink (C) and aqua (D); subcut strips into (56) 3½" squares each C and D.

5. Cut (12) 3⅞" by fabric width strips each blue (E) and green (F); subcut strips into (112) 3⅞" squares. Cut each square in half on one diagonal to make 224 triangles each E and F.

6. Cut one 13⅝" by fabric width strip blue; subcut strip into two 13⅝" squares. Cut each square in half on one diagonal to make four H triangles.

7. Cut (10) 9" by fabric width strips blue; subcut strips into four 9" x 31" K and four 9" x 40" L strips. Set aside remaining two strips to make G units.

8. Cut nine 2½" by fabric width strips yellow for binding.

Completing the Blocks

Note: *All seams are pressed open.*
1. Stitch B to opposite sides of A to make an A-B unit as shown in Figure 1; repeat to make 14 units.

Make 14

Figure 1

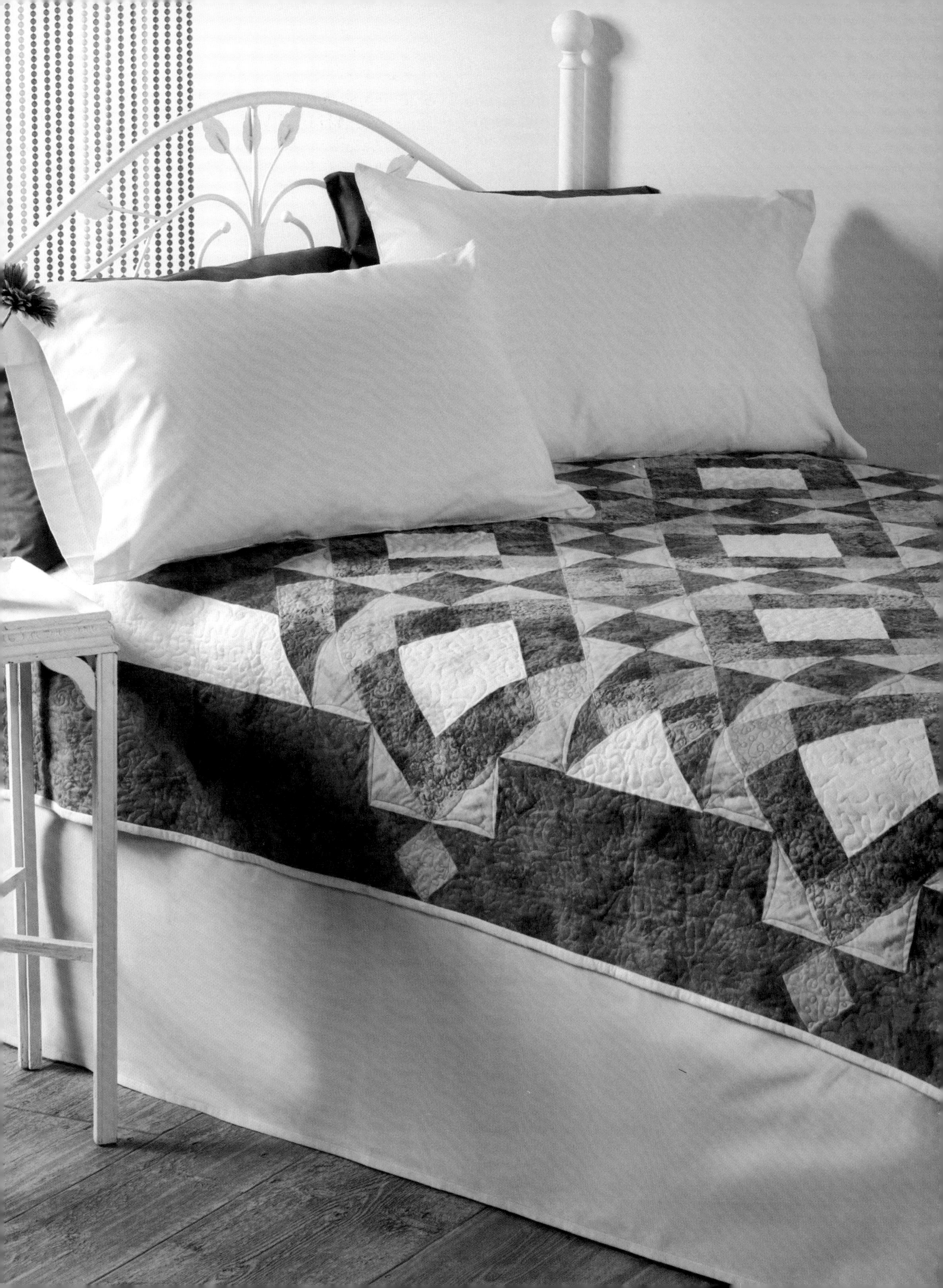

2. Stitch C to one end of B and D to the opposite end to make a C-B-D unit as shown in Figure 2; repeat to make 28 units.

Make 28

Figure 2

3. Stitch a C-B-D unit to opposite sides of an A-B unit to complete a center unit as shown in Figure 3; repeat to make 14 center units.

Make 14

Figure 3

4. Stitch E to F along the diagonal to complete an E-F square; repeat to make 224 squares.

Spring Fling
Placement Diagram 76½" x 102"

5. Join four E-F squares to make E-F units as shown in Figure 4; repeat to make 56 units.

Make 56

Figure 4

6. Stitch an E-F unit to opposite sides of a center unit as shown in Figure 5; repeat to make 14 E-F center units.

Make 14

Figure 5

7. Stitch a D square to one end and a C square to the opposite end of each remaining E-F unit as shown in Figure 6.

Figure 6

8. Stitch a C-D-E-F unit to opposite sides of the E-F-center unit referring to the block drawing for placement to complete one block; repeat to make 14 blocks.

Completing the Quilt

1. Stitch a yellow G strip to a blue G strip with right sides together along length; repeat for two G strip sets. Press seams toward blue strip.

2. Referring to Figure 7, lay a strip set on cutting mat and cut at a 45-degree angle from a blue corner. Measure 26¾" on the blue edge and cut another 45-degree angle to complete a G unit, again referring to Figure 7; repeat with second strip set for two G units.

26¾"

45-degree angle

Figure 7

3. Lay out the blocks with the G units to make rows as shown in Figure 8; join to complete the quilt center.

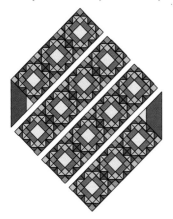

Figure 8

4. Stitch I to H and add J as shown in Figure 9; trim ends of I and J even with edge of H, again referring to Figure 9. Repeat for two H-I-J units and two reversed units.

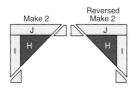

Figure 9

5. Add one each K and L piece to each H-I-J unit as in step 4 to complete two corner units and two reversed corner units referring to Figure 10.

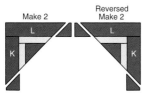

Figure 10

6. Stitch the corner units to the sides of the pieced center to complete the quilt top referring to the Placement Diagram for positioning.

7. Layer, quilt and bind referring to Finishing Your Quilt on page 176.

Dragonfly Rings

Conversation prints add interest to simple designs.

DESIGN BY HOLLY DANIELS

Project Specifications
Skill Level: Confident Beginner
Quilt Size: 48" x 60"
Block Size: 12" x 12"
Number of Blocks: 12

Materials

- ¼ yard light green print
- ⅜ yard each dark pink, dark purple, dark green and dark blue prints
- ½ yard each pink dot, light purple print and yellow tonal
- 1⅔ yards blue dragonfly print
- Backing 54" x 66"
- Batting 54" x 66"
- Neutral-color all-purpose thread
- Hand- or machine-quilting thread
- Basic sewing tools and supplies

Cutting

1. Cut blue dragonfly print along the lengthwise fold to make two 21" x 1⅔-yard lengths. Use one piece to cut block pieces; set aside the second piece for borders.

2. Cut two 3⅜" x 21" strips blue dragonfly print; subcut strips into (12) 3⅜" A squares.

3. Cut two 2⅞" by fabric width strips light green print; subcut strips into (24) 2⅞" squares. Cut each square in half on one diagonal to make 48 B triangles.

4. Cut two 5¼" by fabric width strips each dark green (C) and dark blue (E) prints; subcut strips into (12) 5¼" squares of each fabric. Cut each square on both diagonals to make 48 each C and E triangles.

5. Cut four 2⅞" by fabric width strips yellow tonal; subcut strips into (48) 2⅞" squares. Cut each square in half on one diagonal to make 96 D triangles.

Dragonfly Rings A
12" x 12" Block
Make 4

Dragonfly Rings B
12" x 12" Block
Make 6

Dragonfly Rings C
12" x 12" Block
Make 2

6. Cut seven 2⅞" x 21" strips blue dragonfly print; subcut strips into (48) 2⅞" squares. Cut each square in half on one diagonal to make 96 F triangles.

7. Cut six 4⅞" x 21" strips blue dragonfly print; subcut strips into (24) 4⅞" squares. Cut each square in half on one diagonal to make 48 G triangles.

8. Cut two 4⅞" by fabric width strips each dark purple (H) and dark pink (I) prints; subcut strips into (12) 4⅞" squares each fabric. Cut each square in half on one diagonal to make 24 H and 24 I triangles.

9. Cut two 1½" x 38½" K strips light purple print.

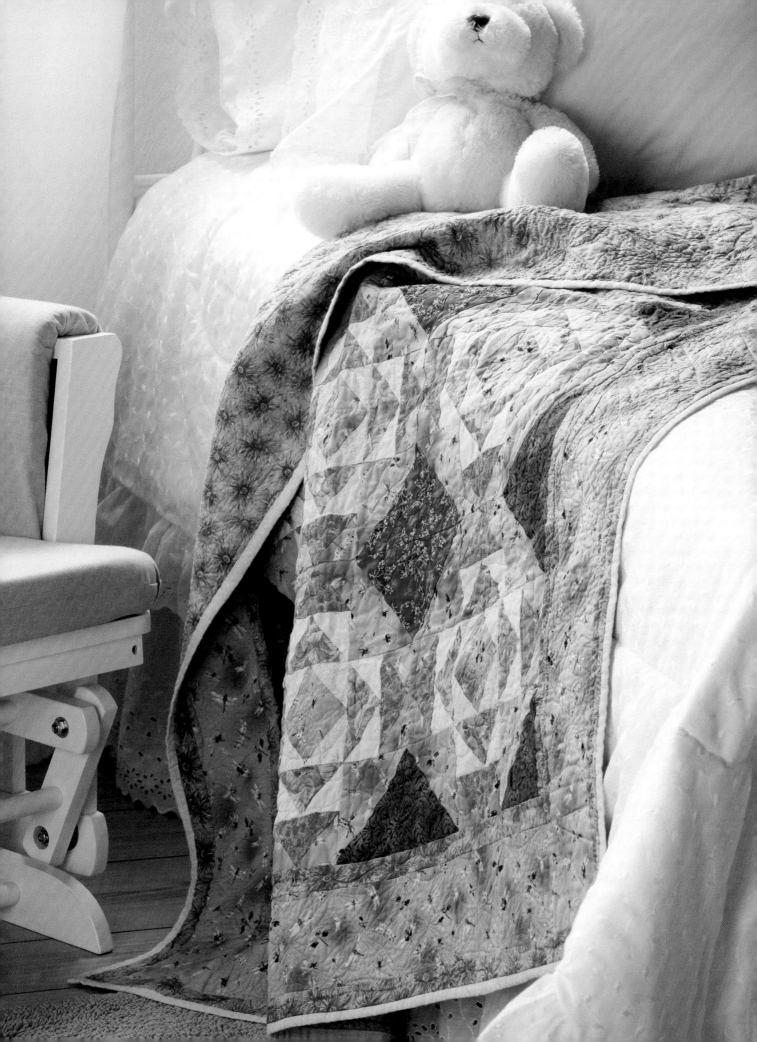

10. Cut eight 1½" by fabric width strips light purple print. Join strips on short ends to make one long strip; press seams open. Subcut strip into four 1½" x 48½" J strips and two 1½" x 58½" N strips.

11. Cut two 4½" x 50½" L strips and two 4½" x 46½" M strips along the length of the blue dragonfly print set aside in step 1.

12. Cut six 2¼" by fabric width strips pink dot for binding.

Completing the Blocks

1. Stitch B to each side of A to make a center unit as shown in Figure 1; press seams toward B. Repeat for 12 center units.

Figure 1

2. Stitch D to the short sides of C to make a C-D unit as shown in Figure 2; press seams toward D. Repeat for 48 C-D units.

Figure 2

3. Stitch F to the short sides of E to make an E-F unit, again referring to Figure 2; press seams toward F. Repeat for 48 E-F units.

4. Join one C-D unit with one E-F unit to complete one side unit as shown in Figure 3; press seams toward E-F unit. Repeat for 48 side units.

Side Unit
Make 48

Figure 3

5. Stitch G to H along the diagonal to complete a purple corner unit as shown in Figure 4; repeat for 24 purple corner units.

Corner Unit
Make 24 each

Figure 4

6. Stitch G to I along the diagonal to complete a pink corner unit, again referring to Figure 4; repeat for 24 pink corner units.

7. To complete one A block, stitch a side unit to opposite sides of a center unit to complete the center row referring to Figure 5; press seams toward the center unit.

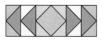

Figure 5

8. Stitch a purple corner unit to opposite sides of a side unit to make the top row referring to Figure 6; press seams toward corner units.

Figure 6

9. Stitch a purple corner unit to one side and a pink corner unit to the opposite side of a side unit to make the bottom row as shown in Figure 7; press seams toward corner units.

Figure 7

10. Join the rows referring to the block drawing to complete one A block; press seams away from the center row.

11. Repeat steps 7–10 to make four A blocks.

12. Repeat steps 7–10 except use two pink corner units for the bottom row to complete six B blocks.

13. Repeat steps 7–10 except use four pink corner units to complete two C blocks.

Completing the Quilt

1. Arrange the completed blocks in four rows of three blocks each referring to the Placement Diagram for positioning. Join blocks in rows; press seams in one direction. Join the rows to complete the pieced center; press seams in one direction.

2. Stitch J strips to opposite sides and K strips to the top and bottom of the pieced center; press seams toward J and K strips.

3. Stitch L strips to opposite sides and M strips to the top and bottom of the pieced center; press seams toward L and M strips.

4. Stitch N strips to opposite sides and J strips to the top and bottom of the pieced center; press seams toward J and N strips.

5. Layer, quilt and bind referring to Finishing Your Quilt on page 176. ■

Dragonfly Rings
Placement Diagram 48" x 60"

Swirling Pinwheels

A simple Pinwheel block comes alive when made
with a variety of fabrics and a lively stripe.

DESIGN BY CHERYL ADAMS

PROJECT SPECIFICATIONS

Skill Level: Beginner
Quilt Size: 49½" x 70½"
Block Size: 9" x 9"
Number of Blocks: 24

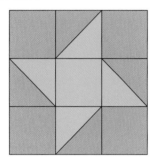

Pinwheel
9" x 9" Block
Make 24

MATERIALS

- ½ yard each 10 assorted prints
- ⅝ yard green print
- ¾ yard black/green stripe
- 1 yard black print
- Backing 55" x 76"
- Batting 55" x 76"
- Neutral-color all-purpose thread
- Quilting thread
- Basic sewing tools and supplies

Cutting

Note: *All the pieces cut for a single set in the steps below
should be cut from one fabric.*

1. Cut 24 sets as follows from the 10 assorted prints
for Pinwheel block star designs: one 3½" A square and
two 3⅞" B squares.

2. Cut 24 sets as follows from the 10 assorted prints for
Pinwheel block backgrounds: two 3⅞" C squares and

four 3½" D squares. Draw a diagonal line from corner
to corner on the wrong side of each C square.

3. Cut one 2" by fabric width strip each from the 10
assorted prints; subcut each strip into (21) 2" squares.

4. From the squares cut in step 3, select four sets of
three matching squares each for corner units, 16 sets
of four matching squares each for end units, and 15
sets of five matching squares each for sashing stars.
Set aside one square from each set for F; draw a
diagonal line from corner to corner on the wrong side
of the remaining squares in each set for E. Set aside
remaining 2" squares for another project.

5. Cut three 9½" by fabric width strips black print;
subcut strips into (58) 2" x 9½" G strips.

6. Cut six 3½" by fabric width strips green/black stripe.
Join strips on short ends, matching stripes to continue
pattern as necessary; press seams open. Subcut strip
into two 3½" x 44" H strips and two 3½" x 71" I strips.

7. Cut six 2¼" by fabric width strips green print
for binding.

Completing the Pinwheel Blocks

1. To complete one Pinwheel block, select one set of
matching A and B pieces, and one set of matching C
and D pieces.

2. With right sides together,
place a C square on top of a B
square; stitch ¼" on each side of
the marked line on C as shown
in Figure 1.

Figure 1

3. Cut apart on the drawn line and press the B-C units
open with the seam toward the darker fabric, again
referring to Figure 1. Repeat with second set of B and
C squares to complete four B-C units.

4. Sew a B-C unit to opposite sides of A as shown in Figure 2 to make the center row; press seams toward A.

Figure 2

Figure 3

5. Sew a D square to opposite sides of a B-C unit to complete the top row as shown in Figure 3; press seams toward D. Repeat for bottom row.

6. Sew the top and bottom rows to the center row to complete one Pinwheel block referring to the block drawing; press seams in one direction. Repeat to make 24 blocks.

7. Repeat steps 1–6 to make 24 blocks.

Completing the Quilt

1. Arrange four blocks with five G sashing strips to make a block row referring to the Placement Diagram for positioning; repeat for six rows.

2. Arrange the matching E and F sets together at the ends and between G pieces to make matching-fabric sashing stars, and end and corner units as shown in Figure 4.

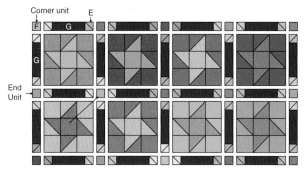

Figure 4

3. Working with one G piece at a time, pin and stitch the E squares on the ends of G as shown in Figure 5; trim seams to ¼" and press E pieces to the right side to complete one E-G sashing strip. Lay the stitched strip back down in its assigned position, referring to Figure 4 and the Placement Diagram, and continue stitching until all sashing units are stitched.

Figure 5

4. To complete a block row, join five E-G sashing strips with four blocks as shown in Figure 6, being careful to

retain the assigned position of each strip; press seams toward E-G units. Repeat for six block rows.

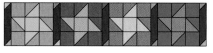

Figure 6

5. Join five F squares with four E-G sashing strips to make a sashing row as shown in Figure 7, being careful to retain the assigned position of each strip; press seams toward E-G units. Repeat for seven sashing rows.

Figure 7

6. Join the sashing rows and the blocks rows to complete the pieced center, again retaining the assigned position of each row; press seams toward sashing rows.

7. Sew an H strip to the top and bottom, and I strips to opposite sides of the pieced center to complete the top; press seams toward H and I strips.

8. Layer, quilt and bind referring to Finishing Your Quilt on page 176. ■

Swirling Pinwheel
Placement Diagram 49½" x 70½"

Jitter Buzz

Jitter Buzz was created in tribute to the designer's friend, Buzz. It is filled with her favorite things—full moons, stars and fish.

DESIGN BY KIM HAZLETT

PROJECT SPECIFICATIONS

Skill Level: Intermediate
Quilt Size: 53¼" x 72⅜"
Block Size: 13½" x 13½"
Number of Blocks: 8

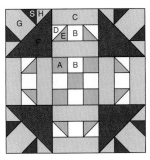

Jitter
13½" x 13½" Block
Make 6

Buzz
13½" x 13½" Block
Make 2

MATERIALS

- ⅓ yard dark blue print
- ⅜ yard total gold scraps
- ½ yard total dark red scraps
- ½ yard total medium red scraps
- ½ yard total medium green scraps
- ½ yard dark red tonal
- ⅝ yard total cream scraps
- ¾ yard total dark green scraps
- 1½ yards total tan scraps
- 2 yards dark green tonal
- Backing 60" x 79"
- Batting 60" x 79"
- Neutral-color all-purpose thread
- Quilting thread
- Template material
- Basic sewing tools and supplies

PROJECT NOTE

The quilt shown was made with scrap fabric strips. Total yardage is given if planned fabrics will be used. The number of strips needed from each color family is given for quick cutting. If scrap pieces are used instead of scrap strips or yardage, cut the total number of pieces needed for each piece.

Cutting

1. Cut one 3⅝" by fabric width strip dark blue print; subcut strip into eight 3⅝" O squares.

2. Cut one 2⅛" by fabric width strip dark blue print; subcut strip into four 2⅛" Q squares.

3. Cut two 5" by fabric width strips dark red scraps; layer strips right sides together. Prepare template for piece K using pattern given; place K on strips and cut 24 each K and KR pieces from the strips as shown in Figure 1.

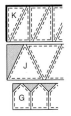

Figure 1

4. Cut two 5⅜" by fabric width strips medium red scraps; subcut strips into (12) 5⅜" squares. Cut each square in half on one diagonal to make 24 F triangles.

5. Cut two 2⅜" by fabric width strips medium green scraps; subcut strips into (24) 2⅜" squares. Cut each square in half on one diagonal to make 48 E triangles.

6. Cut three 2" by fabric width A strips medium green scraps.

7. Cut one 3⅛" by fabric width strip gold scrap; subcut strip into (13) 3⅛" squares. Cut each square in half on one diagonal to make 26 I triangles.

8. Cut one 2½" by fabric width strip gold scrap; subcut strip into four 2½" squares. Cut each square in half on one diagonal to make eight U triangles.

9. Cut seven 2" by fabric width strips dark red tonal. Join strips on short ends to make one long strip; press seams open. Subcut strip into two 2" x 75" W strips and two 2" x 55" X strips.

10. Cut five 2" by fabric width B strips cream scraps; subcut two strips into (24) 2" B squares. Set aside remaining strips for A-B strip sets.

11. Cut two 2⅜" by fabric width strips cream scraps; subcut strips into (24) 2⅜" squares. Cut each square in half on one diagonal to make 48 D triangles.

12. Cut one 5⅜" by fabric width strip dark green scrap; subcut strip into seven 5⅜" squares. Cut each square in half on one diagonal to make 14 N triangles.

13. Cut one 3⅛" by fabric width strip dark green scrap; subcut strip into seven 3⅛" squares. Cut each square in half on one diagonal to make 14 M triangles.

14. Cut one 4" by fabric width strip dark green scrap; subcut strip into (10) 4" squares. Cut each square in half on one diagonal to make 20 P triangles.

15. Cut two 2⅜" by fabric width strips dark green scraps; subcut strips into (24) 2⅜" squares. Cut each square in half on one diagonal to make 48 S triangles.

16. Cut one 2½" by fabric width strip dark green scrap; subcut strip into (10) 2½" squares. Cut each square in half on one diagonal to make 20 R triangles.

17. Cut seven 6½" by fabric width strips dark green tonal. Join strips on short ends to make one long strip; press seams open. Subcut strip into two 6½" x 75" Y strips and two 6½" x 55" Z strips.

18. Cut seven 2¼" by fabric width strips dark green tonal for binding.

19. Cut three 3⅛" by fabric width strips tan scraps; subcut strips into (31) 3⅛" squares. Cut each square in half on one diagonal to make 62 L triangles.

20. Cut two 5" by fabric width strips tan scraps. Prepare a template for piece J; cut 24 J pieces from the strips, again referring to Figure 1.

21. Cut two 3¾" by fabric width strips tan scraps. Prepare a template for piece G; cut 24 G pieces from strips, again referring to Figure 1.

22. Cut six 2" by fabric width strips tan scraps; subcut strips into (48) 2" x 5" C rectangles.

23. Cut two 2⅜" by fabric width strips tan scraps; subcut strips into (24) 2⅜" squares. Cut each square in half on one diagonal to make 48 H triangles.

24. Cut one 2½" by fabric width strip tan scrap; subcut strip into (10) 2½" squares. Cut each square in half on one diagonal to make 20 T triangles.

Completing the Jitter Blocks

1. Stitch a B strip between two A strips with right sides together along the length; press seams toward A strips.

2. Stitch an A strip between two B strips with right sides together along the length; press seams toward A strips.

3. Subcut the A-B-A strip set into (12) 2" segments and the B-A-B strip set into six 2" B-A-B segments as shown in Figure 2.

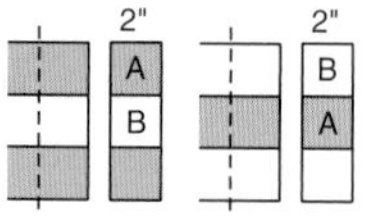

Figure 2

4. Stitch a B-A-B segment between two A-B-A segments to complete a Nine-Patch unit as shown in Figure 3; repeat to make six units. Press seams away from the B-A-B segments.

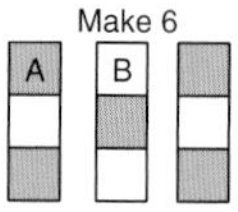

Figure 3

5. Stitch D to E along the diagonal to make a D-E unit as shown in Figure 4; press seam toward E. Repeat to make 48 D-E units.

Make 48

Figure 4

6. Join two D-E units with a B square as shown in Figure 5; press seams toward B. Repeat to make 24 B-D-E units.

Figure 5

7. Stitch C to top and bottom of each B-D-E unit as shown in Figure 6 to make 24 side units; press seams toward C.

Figure 6

8. Stitch H to S as shown in Figure 7; repeat to make 24 H-S and 24 reversed H-S units, again referring to Figure 7. Press seam toward S.

Figure 7

9. Stitch an H-S unit and a reversed H-S unit to G as shown in Figure 8; press seams toward G. Repeat to make 24 units.

Figure 8

10. Stitch F to a G-H-S unit to complete a corner unit as shown in Figure 9; press seam toward F. Repeat to make 24 corner units.

Figure 9

11. To complete one Jitter block, stitch a corner unit to opposite sides of a side unit to complete the top row referring to Figure 10; repeat to make the bottom row. Press seams toward the side units.

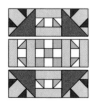

Figure 10

12. Stitch a side unit to opposite sides of a Nine-Patch unit to complete the center row, again referring to Figure 10; press seams toward the side units.

13. Join the rows to complete one Jitter block, again referring to Figure 10; press seams toward the center row.

14. Repeat steps 11–13 to make six Jitter blocks.

Completing the Buzz Blocks

1. Stitch I to each side of O to complete a center unit as shown in Figure 11; press seams toward I. Repeat to make two center units.

Figure 11

2. Stitch K and KR to J as shown in Figure 12; repeat to make 24 J-K units. Press seams toward K and KR. Set aside 16 units for quilt side and corner units.

Figure 12

3. Stitch L to M and add L to each M side to complete an L-M unit as shown in Figure 13; repeat to make 14 L-M units. Press seams toward M and then L.

Figure 13

4. Stitch N to each L-M unit to complete a corner unit, again referring to Figure 13; repeat to make 14 block corner units. Press seams toward N. Set aside six units for quilt side units.

5. To complete one Buzz block, stitch a J-K unit between two block corner units to make the top row referring to Figure 14; repeat to make the bottom row. Press seams toward the corner units.

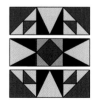

Figure 14

6. Stitch a J-K unit to opposite sides of the center unit to make the center row, again referring to Figure 14; press seams toward the center unit.

7. Stitch the center row between the top and bottom rows to complete one Buzz block, again referring to Figure 14; press seams away from the center row.

8. Repeat steps 5–7 to make two Buzz blocks.

Completing the Side & Corner Units

1. Stitch R to T and add L as shown in Figure 15; repeat to make 10 L-R-T units and 10 reversed L-R-T units, again referring to Figure 15. Press seams toward R and then L.

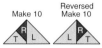

Figure 15

2. Stitch P to each L-R-T and reversed L-R-T unit as shown in Figure 16; press seams toward P.

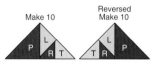

Figure 16

3. Stitch I to three sides of O as shown in Figure 17; press seams toward I. Repeat to make six I-O units.

Figure 17

4. Join one L-M-N corner unit and one I-O unit with two J-K units and one each L-R-T-P and reversed L-R-T-P unit referring to Figure 18; press seams in the direction of the arrows.

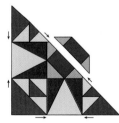

Figure 18

5. Trim the excess I-O unit even with the angle of the L-R-T-P units to complete a side unit, again referring to Figure 18. Repeat to make six side units.

6. Stitch U to two adjacent sides of Q as shown in Figure 19; press seams toward Q. Repeat to make four Q-U units.

Figure 19

7. Stitch an L-R-T-P unit and a reversed L-R-T-P unit to opposite sides of a J-K unit and add a Q-U unit to complete a corner unit referring to Figure 20; repeat to make four corner units. Press seams in direction of arrows, again referring to Figure 20.

Figure 20

Completing the Quilt

1. Arrange the pieced blocks with the side and corner units in diagonal rows as shown in Figure 21. Join in rows; press seams in adjacent rows in opposite directions.

Figure 21

2. Join the rows to complete the pieced center; press seams in one direction.

3. Stitch a W strip to a Y strip with right sides together along the length. Repeat to make two W-Y and two X-Z strips; press seams toward Y and Z strips.

4. Center and stitch a W-Y strip to opposite long sides and X-Z strips to the top and bottom of the pieced center, mitering corners; press seams toward the pieced strips.

5. Trim mitered seams to ¼"; press seams open.

6. Layer, quilt and bind referring to Finishing Your Quilt on page 176. ■

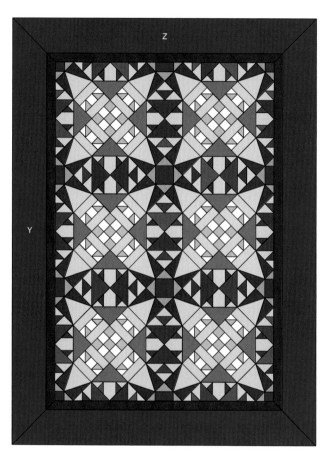

Jitter Buzz
Placement Diagram 53¼" x 72³/₈"

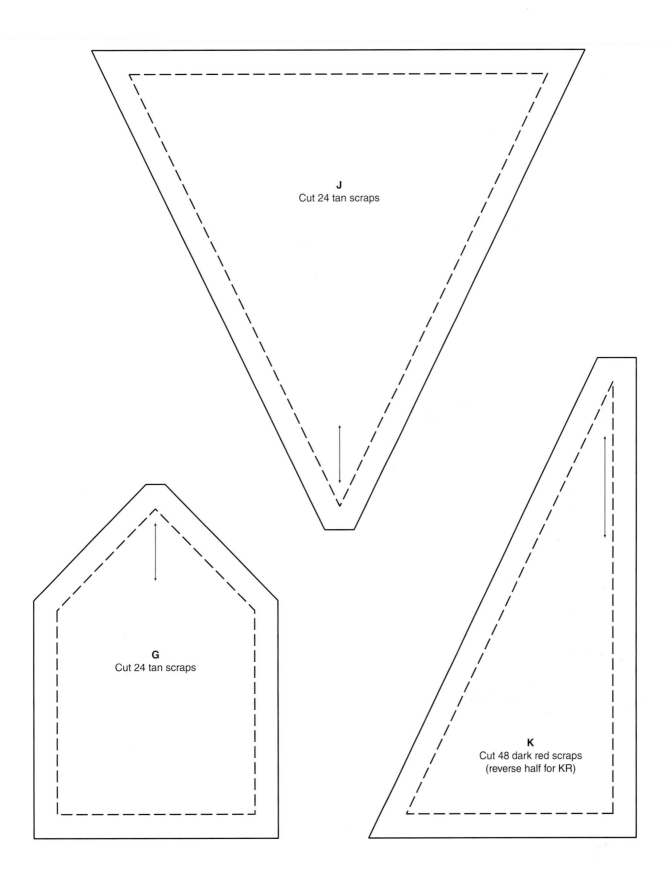

J
Cut 24 tan scraps

G
Cut 24 tan scraps

K
Cut 48 dark red scraps
(reverse half for KR)

Cartwheels

Batik flannels add even more of a soft touch to a simple pieced quilt.

DESIGN BY LUCY A. FAZELY & MICHAEL L. BURNS

PROJECT SPECIFICATIONS

Skill Level: Beginner
Quilt Size: 49½" x 62"
Block Size: 12½" x 12½"
Number of Blocks: 12

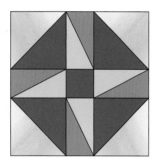

Cartwheel
12½" x 12½" Block
Make 12

MATERIALS

- ⅜ yard navy/teal flannel
- ½ yard bright green flannel
- ½ yard dark teal flannel
- ¾ yard light multicolored flannel
- ⅞ yard dark blue flannel
- 1⅜ yards flannel print
- Backing 55" x 68"
- Batting 55" x 68"
- Neutral-color all-purpose thread
- Quilting thread
- Basting spray
- Template material
- Basic sewing tools and supplies

Cutting

1. Cut four 3" by fabric width strips each dark teal (A) and bright green (B).

2. Prepare template for A/B. Place the template on the strips as shown in Figure 1; cut 48 each A and B pieces.

Figure 1

3. Cut one 3" by fabric width strip dark blue; subcut strip into (12) 3" C squares.

4. Cut four 5⅞" by fabric width strips each dark blue (D) and light multicolored (E); subcut strips into (24) 5⅞" each D and E squares. Cut each D and E square in half on one diagonal to make 48 each D and E triangles.

5. Cut five 2" by fabric width strips navy/teal. Join strips on short ends to make one long strip; subcut into two 2" x 50½" F and two 2" x 41" G strips.

6. Cut six 5" by fabric width strips flannel print. Join strips on short ends to make one long strip; subcut into two 5" x 53½" H and two 5" x 50" I strips.

7. Cut six 2½" by fabric width strips flannel print for binding.

Piecing the Blocks

1. To piece one block, stitch A to B as shown in Figure 2; press seam toward A. Repeat to make four units.

Make 4

Figure 2

2. Stitch D to E along the diagonal; press seams toward D. Repeat for four D-E units.

3. Join two A-B units with C to make center row as shown in Figure 3; press seams toward C.

Figure 3

4. Join two D-E units with an A-B unit to make a top row as shown in Figure 4; press seams toward D-E. Repeat to make a bottom row.

Make 2

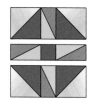

Figure 4

5. Join the pieced rows to complete one Cartwheel block as shown in Figure 5; press seams toward center row.

Figure 5

6. Repeat steps 1–5 to make 12 blocks.

Completing the Quilt

1. Join three blocks to make a row; press seams in one direction. Repeat to make four rows.

2. Join the rows to complete the pieced center; press seams in one direction.

3. Stitch F to opposite long sides and G to the top and bottom of the pieced center; press seams toward F and G.

4. Stitch H to opposite long sides and I to the top and bottom of the pieced center; press seams toward H and I to complete the pieced top.

5. Layer, quilt and bind referring to Finishing Your Quilt on page 176. ◼

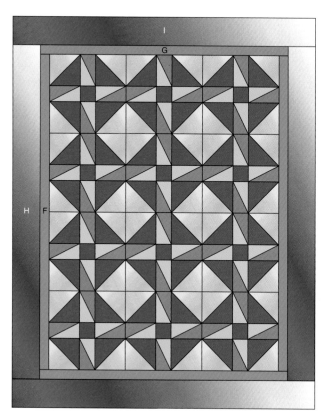

Cartwheels
Placement Diagram 49½" x 62"

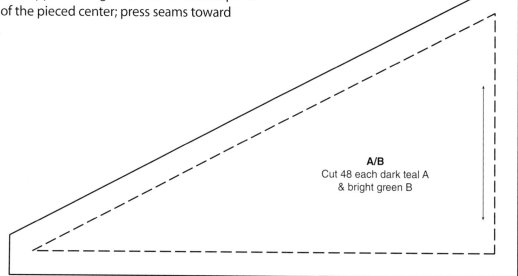

A/B
Cut 48 each dark teal A
& bright green B

Origins of Nines

Nine-Patch blocks are the foundation of many classic quilts; page through this chapter to see the diversity of the simple Nine-Patch.

Four-in-Nine-Patch Zigzag

Whether you choose to make a planned arrangement or a scrappy version, this simple quilt top can be made in a day.

DESIGN BY BARBARA DOUGLAS
QUILTMAKER CANDY ROGERS

PROJECT SPECIFICATIONS

Skill Level: Beginner
Quilt Size: 58" x 70"
Block Size: 4" x 4"
Number of Blocks: 70

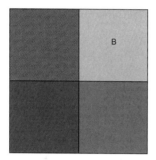

Four-Patch
4" x 4" Block
Make 70

MATERIALS

- ¼ yard each 4 coordinating brown/green/gray prints
- 1¼ yards black tonal
- 1¼ yards brown print
- 1⅜ yards cream tonal
- Backing 64" x 76"
- Batting 64" x 76"
- Neutral-color all-purpose thread
- Quilting thread
- Basic sewing tools and supplies

Cutting

1. Cut three 2½" by fabric width strips from each coordinating brown/green/gray print; subcut strips into a total of (190) 2½" B squares.

2. Cut three 2½" by fabric width black tonal strips; subcut strips into (44) 2½" B squares.

3. Cut six 2½" by fabric width black tonal H/I strips.

4. Cut seven 2¼" by fabric width black tonal strips for binding.

5. Cut three 2½" by fabric width brown print strips; subcut strips into (46) 2½" B squares.

6. Cut six 5½" by fabric width brown print J/K strips.

7. Cut (10) 4½" by fabric width cream tonal strips; subcut strips into (50) 4½" A squares, four 4½" x 8½" G rectangles, six 4½" x 12½" E rectangles and two 4½" x 16½" F rectangles.

Completing the Four-Patch Blocks

1. Randomly select four different B squares.

2. Join two B squares; press seam in one direction. Repeat to make two B units.

3. Join the two B units with seams in opposite directions to complete one Four-Patch block referring to the block drawing; press seam in one direction.

4. Repeat steps 1–3 to complete 70 Four-Patch blocks.

Completing the Pieced Units

1. Join one Four-Patch block with two A squares to make an A unit as shown in Figure 1; press seams toward the A squares. Repeat to make 24 A units.

A Unit
Make 24

Figure 1

2. Join three Four-Patch blocks to make a B unit as shown in Figure 2; press seams in one direction. Repeat to make 12 B units.

B Unit
Make 12

Figure 2

C Unit
Make 10

Figure 3

3. Join one B unit and two A units as shown in Figure 3 to complete a C unit; repeat to make 10 C units. Press seams away from the B unit.

4. Join one B unit and one A unit to complete a D unit as shown in Figure 4; press seam toward the A unit. Repeat to make two D units. *Note: You will have two remaining A units.*

D Unit
Make 2

Figure 4

Completing the Quilt

1. Join three C units as shown in Figure 5 to complete a C row; press seams in one direction. Repeat to make two C rows.

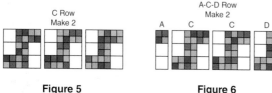

C Row
Make 2

Figure 5

A-C-D Row
Make 2

A   C   C   D

Figure 6

2. Join one each A and D units and two C units to make an A-C-D row as shown in Figure 6; press seams in one direction. Repeat to make two A-C-D rows.

3. Referring to Figure 7, arrange and join the rows to complete the pieced center; press seams in one direction.

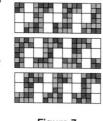

4. Join two E strips with two Four-Patch blocks and one F strip to make a side strip as shown in Figure 8; press seams toward E and F strips. Repeat to make two side strips.

Figure 7

Make 2

E   F

Figure 8

5. Sew a side strip to opposite long sides of the pieced center; press seams toward side strips.

6. Join one A square, one E strip, two G strips and three Four-Patch blocks to make the top strip as

shown in Figure 9; press seams toward E and G strips, and away from A. Repeat to make the bottom strip.

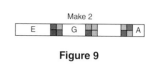

Make 2

E   G   A

Figure 9

7. Referring to the Placement Diagram for positioning, sew the top and bottom strips to the pieced center; press seams toward strips.

8. Join the H/I strips with right sides together on short ends to make one long strip; press seams open. Subcut strip into two 56½" H strips and two 48½" I strips.

9. Sew H strips to opposite long sides and I strips to the top and bottom of the pieced center; press seams toward H and I strips.

10. Join the J/K strips with right sides together on short ends to make one long strip; press seams open. Subcut strip into two 60½" J strips and two 58½" K strips.

11. Sew J strips to opposite long sides and K strips to the top and bottom of the pieced center to complete the pieced top; press seams toward J and K strips.

12. Layer, quilt and bind referring to Finishing Your Quilt on page 176. ■

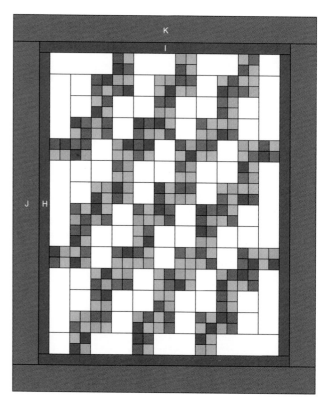

Four-in-Nine-Patch Zigzag
Placement Diagram 58" x 70"

The Harvester

Squirrels store up acorns for the winter in this scrappy autumn quilt.

DESIGN BY MARIA UMHEY

PROJECT SPECIFICATIONS

Skill Level: Intermediate
Quilt Size: 63" x 63"
Block Size: 7½" x 7½"
Number of Blocks: 25

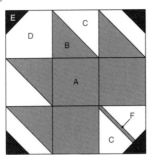

Maple Leaf
7½" x 7½" Block
Make 12

Harvester
7½" x 7½" Block
Make 1

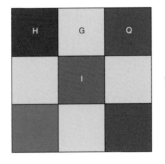

Nine-Patch
7½" x 7½" Block
Make 12

MATERIALS

- Assorted brown and dark green scraps
- 12 fat eighths assorted autumn-color prints
- 12 fat eighths assorted cream prints
- ¼ yard dark red print
- ¼ yard brown/pink print
- 1 yard rust print
- 1⅛ yards tan print
- 1¼ yards brown/rust print
- Backing 69" x 69"
- Batting 69" x 69"
- Neutral-color all-purpose thread
- Brown thread for appliqué
- Quilting thread
- ¼ yard fusible web
- ¼ yard fabric stabilizer
- Basic sewing tools and supplies

Cutting

1. Cut (36) 3" H squares assorted brown scraps.

2. Cut (36) 3" Q squares assorted dark green scraps.

3. From each autumn-color print fat eighth, cut three 3" A squares, one ¾" x 4" F strip and two 3⅜" squares. Cut the 3⅜" squares in half on one diagonal to make four B triangles each autumn-color print.

4. From each cream print fat eighth, cut one 3" D square and three 3⅜" squares. Cut the 3⅜" squares in half on one diagonal to make six C triangles each cream print.

5. Cut one 8" J square from one of the cream prints.

6. Cut two 3" by fabric width dark red print strips; subcut strips into (24) 3" I squares.

7. Cut three 1¾" by fabric width brown/pink print strips; subcut strips into (68) 1¾" E squares.

8. Cut five 2¼" by fabric width rust print M/N strips.

9. Cut seven 2¼" by fabric width rust print strips for binding.

10. Cut one 5½" by fabric width tan print strip; subcut strip into four 5½" L squares.

11. Cut (10) 3" by fabric width tan print strips; subcut strips into (84) 3" G squares and (16) 3" x 8" K rectangles.

12. Cut six 6½" by fabric width brown/rust print O/P strips.

Completing the Harvester Block

1. Trace appliqué patterns onto the paper side of the fusible web as directed on pattern; cut out shapes, leaving a margin around each one.

2. Fuse shapes to the wrong side of fabrics as directed; cut out shapes on traced lines. Remove paper backing.

3. Fold and crease J to mark horizontal and vertical centers.

4. Draw a diagonal line from corner to corner on each E square; select four E squares for Harvester block and set aside remainder for Maple Leaf blocks.

5. Place an E square on each corner of J and stitch on the marked line as shown in Figure 1; trim seam to ¼" and press E to the right side to complete the E-J unit, again referring to Figure 1.

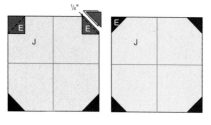

Figure 1

6. Arrange and fuse the squirrel and acorns to the E-J unit, matching the center of J with the positioning center mark on the squirrel.

7. Cut a 7" square fabric stabilizer; pin to the wrong side of the fused E-J square.

8. Using brown thread and a close zigzag stitch, stitch around the acorn and squirrel shapes to complete the block; remove fabric stabilizer.

Completing the Nine-Patch Blocks

1. Referring to the Nine-Patch block drawing, to complete one block join one each H and Q squares with one G square to make top row; press seams toward H and Q squares. Repeat to make a bottom row.

2. Join two G squares with one I square to make a center row; press seams toward the I square.

3. Join the top and bottom rows to the center row to complete one Nine-Patch block; press seams in one direction.

4. Repeat steps 1–3 to complete 12 Nine-Patch blocks.

Completing the Maple Leaf Blocks

1. For one Maple Leaf block, select same fabric for three A, four B and one F; same fabric for six C and one D; and four E.

2. Center and sew C triangles to opposite sides of F as shown in Figure 2; press seams toward F. Trim the C-F unit to 3" square with F centered diagonally, again referring to Figure 2.

Figure 2

3. Sew C to B along the diagonal; press seam toward B. Repeat to make four B-C units.

4. Join two B-C units with D to make the top row as shown in Figure 3; press seams toward D.

Figure 3

5. Join one B-C unit with two A squares to make the center row as shown in Figure 4; press seams toward outer A.

Figure 4

6. Join one B-C unit with one each A square and C-F unit to complete the bottom row as shown in Figure 5; press seams toward the B-C unit.

Figure 5

7. Sew the top row to the center row and add the bottom row referring to Figure 6; press seams in one direction.

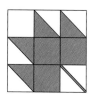

Figure 6

8. Place and stitch E on each corner of the pieced unit, stitching on the marked line as shown in Figure 7; trim seam to ¼" and press E to the right side to complete one Maple Leaf block.

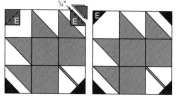

Figure 7

9. Repeat steps 1–8 to complete 12 Maple Leaf blocks.

Completing the Quilt

1. Sew G between H and Q to complete a G-H-Q row as shown in Figure 8; press seams toward H and Q. Repeat to make six each G-H-Q rows and reverse G-H-Q rows.

Figure 8

2. Sew I between two G squares to complete a G-I row; press seams toward I. Repeat to make 12 G-I rows.

3. Join one G-I row with one G-H-Q row to complete a side unit referring to Figure 9; repeat to make six side units and six reverse side units.

Figure 9

4. Referring to Figure 10, place E on two corners of K; sew on the marked line on E. Trim seam to ¼" and press E to the right side to complete an E-K unit, again referring to Figure 10. Repeat to make eight E-K units.

Figure 10

5. Sew an E-K unit to K to make a K unit as shown in Figure 11; press seam toward K. Repeat to make eight K units.

Figure 11

6. Join two K units with three reverse side units and two L squares to make the top row as shown in Figure 12; press seams toward K units. Repeat to make the bottom row.

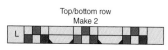

Figure 12

7. Join two side units with two Nine-Patch blocks and three Maple Leaf blocks to make an X row as shown in Figure 13; press seams toward Nine-Patch blocks and side units. Repeat to make three X rows. ***Note:*** *Be careful to position the brown and green corners of the Nine-Patch blocks as shown in the figures to create the "bow-tie" pattern in the quilt.*

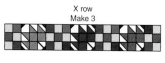

Figure 13

8. Join two Maple Leaf blocks, three Nine-Patch blocks and two K units to make a Y row, referring to Figure 14; press seams toward Nine-Patch blocks.

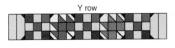

Y row

Figure 14

9. Join one Maple Leaf block, one Harvester block, three Nine-Patch blocks and two K units to make a Z row referring to Figure 15; press seams toward Nine-Patch blocks.

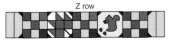

Z row

Figure 15

10. Join the X, Y and Z rows with the top and bottom rows to complete the pieced center referring to the Placement Diagram for positioning; press seams in one direction.

11. Join M/N strips with right sides together on short ends to make one long strip; press seams open. Subcut strip into two 2¼" x 48" M strips and two 2¼" x 51½" N strips.

12. Sew M strips to opposite sides and N strips to the top and bottom of the pieced center; press seams toward M and N strips.

13. Join the O/P strips with right sides together on short ends to make one long strip; press seams open. Subcut strip into two 6½" x 51½" O strips and two 6½" x 63½" P strips.

14. Sew O strips to opposite sides and P strips to the top and bottom of the pieced center to complete the pieced top; press seams toward O and P strips.

15. Layer, quilt and bind referring to Finishing Your Quilt on page 176. ∎

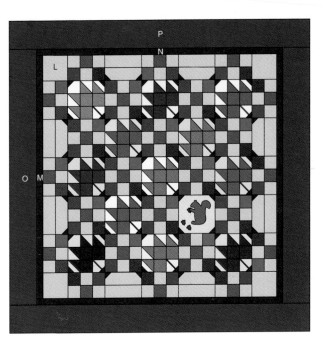

The Harvester
Placement Diagram 63" x 63"

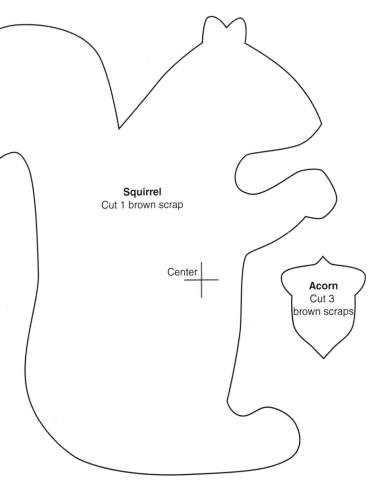

Squirrel
Cut 1 brown scrap

Center

Acorn
Cut 3
brown scraps

Wolf Song

Whether you use a wolf panel or another panel in the center of this quilt, it is a striking example of the variety a preprint panel can bring to a quilt.

DESIGN BY LUCY A. FAZELY & MICHAEL L. BURNS

PROJECT SPECIFICATIONS

Skill Level: Intermediate
Quilt Size: 44" x 56"
Block Size: 10" x 10"
Number of Blocks: 8

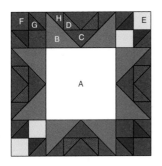

Wolf Star
10" x 10" Block
Make 8

PROJECT NOTES

This pattern uses the Wolf Song fabric collection from Exclusively Quilters and may no longer be available. Choose one of the many pretty preprint panels with coordinating yardage available to quilters today, and showcase them in this pattern.

The framed preprint panel area in this quilt is 20" x 20". To use another panel size in this quilt remember to select a square design, unless you want wider borders on the sides than on the top and bottom. If your preprint panel measures just 12" x 12" finished, you need to make up the 8" difference by adding borders around the panel. You could add 1½"- and 2½"-wide finished borders all around to make the panel finish at 20" x 20".

MATERIALS

- 1 Wolf Song pillow panel 17½" x 17½"
- ¼ yard each light green, brown and dark green tonals
- ½ yard green fern print
- ⅞ yard forest scene print
- 1 yard wolf scene print
- 1⅞ yards black tonal
- Backing 50" x 62"
- Batting 50" x 62"
- Neutral-color all-purpose thread
- Quilting thread
- Quilt basting spray
- Basic sewing tools and supplies

Cutting

1. If needed, trim pillow panel to 17½" square for I.

2. Cut two 1¾" by fabric width light green tonal strips; subcut strips into (32) 1¾" E squares.

3. Cut two 2⅛" by fabric width brown tonal strips; subcut strips into (32) 2⅛" squares. Cut each square in half on one diagonal to make 64 D triangles.

4. Cut two 2⅛" by fabric width dark green tonal strips; subcut strips into (32) 2⅛" squares. Cut each square in half on one diagonal to make 64 G triangles.

5. Cut three 3⅜" by fabric width green fern print strips; subcut strips into (32) 3⅜" squares. Cut each square in half on one diagonal to make 64 B triangles.

6. Cut one 10⅞" by fabric width forest scene print strips; subcut strip into two 10⅞" squares. Cut each square in half on one diagonal to make 4 L triangles.

7. Cut two 6½" x 40½" forest scene print N strips.

8. Fussy-cut eight 5½" A squares with a wolf motif centered in each square from wolf scene print.

9. Cut one 10⅞" by fabric width black tonal strip; subcut strip into two 10⅞" squares. Cut each square in half on one diagonal to make 4 M triangles.

10. Cut two 3¾" by fabric width black tonal strips; subcut strips into (16) 3¾" squares. Cut on both diagonals to make 64 C triangles.

11. Cut four 2⅛" by fabric width black tonal strips; subcut strips into (64) 2⅛" squares. Cut in half on one diagonal to make 128 H triangles.

12. Cut two 1¾" by fabric width black tonal strips; subcut strips into (32) 1¾" F squares.

13. Cut two 2" by fabric width black tonal strips; subcut strips into two 2" x 17½" J strips and two 2" x 20½" K strips.

14. Cut five 2½" by fabric width black tonal O/P strips.

15. Cut six 2¼" by fabric width black tonal strips for binding.

Completing the Wolf Star Blocks

1. Sew H to G along the diagonal to make a G-H unit; press seam toward H. Repeat to make 64 G-H units.

2. Sew a G-H unit to an E square as shown in Figure 1; press seams toward E. Repeat to make 32 G-H-E units.

Figure 1

3. Join two G-H-E units to make a green corner unit as shown in Figure 2; press seam in one direction. Repeat to make 16 green corner units.

Figure 2

4. Repeat steps 2 and 3 with G-H units and F to make 16 black corner units referring to Figure 3.

Figure 3

5. Sew D to each short side of C to make a C-D unit as shown in Figure 4; press seams toward D. Repeat to make 32 C-D units.

Figure 4

6. Sew C to each C-D unit to make 32 C-C-D units referring to Figure 5; press seams toward C.

Figure 5

7. Add an H triangle to each D side of each C-C-D unit to make 32 triangle units as shown in Figure 6; press seams toward H.

Figure 6

8. Sew a B triangle to each C-H side of each triangle unit to complete 32 side units as shown in Figure 7; press seams toward B.

Figure 7

9. To make one Wolf Star block, sew a side unit to opposite sides of A to make a center row as shown in Figure 8; press seams toward A.

Figure 8

10. Sew a black corner unit to one end and a green corner unit to the opposite end of two side units to make the top and bottom rows referring to Figure 9 and the block drawing; press seams toward corner units.

Figure 9

11. Sew the top and bottom rows to opposite sides of the center row to complete one Wolf Star block; press seams toward the center row.

12. Repeat steps 9–11 to complete eight Wolf Star blocks referring to the Placement Diagram for positioning of the side units, and top and bottom rows to keep the wolf print upright in the A squares.

Completing the Quilt

1. Sew a J strip to opposite sides and K strips to the top and bottom of the I panel square to make the framed center; press seams toward J and K strips.

2. Join two Wolf Star blocks to make a block row as shown in Figure 10; press seam in one direction. Repeat to make four block rows, referring to the Placement Diagram for positioning of blocks in rows.

Figure 10

3. Sew a block row to opposite sides of the framed center to make the center row; press seams toward J strips.

4. Sew M to L along the diagonal; press seam toward M. Repeat to make four M-L units.

5. Sew an M-L unit to opposite ends of each remaining block row as shown in Figure 11; press seams toward M-L units.

Figure 11

6. Sew an M-L/block row to the top and bottom of the center row referring to the Placement Diagram for positioning; press seams toward the center row.

7. Sew N strips to the top and bottom of the pieced center; press seams toward N strips. **Note:** *The fabric used for N in the sample is directional. If your fabric is directional be sure to keep the fabric upright if that is important in the finished quilt.*

8. Join the O/P strips on short ends to make one long strip; press seams open. Subcut the strip into two 2½" x 52½" O strips and two 2½" x 44½" P strips.

9. Sew an O strip to opposite long sides and P strips to the top and bottom of the pieced center; press seams toward O and P strips to complete the pieced top.

10. Layer, quilt and bind referring to Finishing Your Quilt on page 176. ■

Wolf Song
Placement Diagram 44" x 56"

Mystic Chords of Memory

"I am loath to close. We are not enemies, but friends. We must not be enemies. Though passion may have strained, it must not break our bonds of affection. The mystic chords of memory, stretching from every battlefield and patriot grave to every living heart and hearthstone all over this broad land, will yet swell the chorus of the Union, when again touched, as surely they will be, by the better angels of our nature."—Abraham Lincoln, First Inaugural Address, March 4, 1861

DESIGN BY MARIA UMHEY

PROJECT SPECIFICATIONS

Skill Level: Intermediate
Quilt Size: 81" x 81"
Block Size: 9" x 9"
Number of Blocks: 64

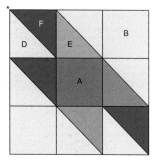

Block A
9" x 9" Block
Make 4

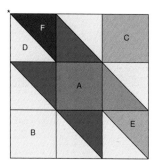

Block B
9" x 9" Block
Make 12

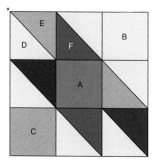

Block C
9" x 9" Block
Make 12

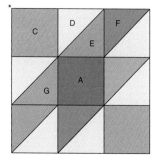

Block D
9" x 9" Block
Make 16

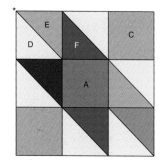

Block E
9" x 9" Block
Make 12

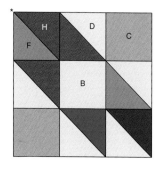

Block F
9" x 9" Block
Make 4

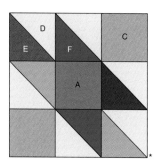

Block G
9" x 9" Block
Make 4

- ⅓ yard red/white print
- ½ yard each 4 brown prints
- ⅝ yard cream/red print
- ⅝ yard each 4 blue prints
- 1 yard brown leaf print
- 1¼ yards royal/navy print
- 3 yards cream tonal
- Backing 87" x 87"
- Batting 87" x 87"
- Neutral-color all-purpose thread
- Red machine-embroidery thread
- Quilting thread
- ¾ yard 12"-wide fusible web
- ¾ yard fabric stabilizer
- Basic sewing tools and supplies

Cutting

1. Cut one 3⅞" by fabric width red/white print strip; subcut six 3⅞" squares. Cut squares in half on one diagonal to make 12 H triangles.

2. Cut one 3½" by fabric width red/white print strip; subcut strip into (11) 3½" K squares.

3. Cut two 3⅞" by fabric width strips from each brown print; subcut strips into a total of (56) 3⅞" squares from strips. Cut each square in half on one diagonal to make 112 E triangles.

4. Cut one 3½" by fabric width strip from each of four brown prints; subcut strip into (12) 3½" K squares from each strip.

5. Cut two 3⅞" by fabric width cream/red print strips; subcut strips into (16) 3⅞" squares. Cut each square in half on one diagonal to make 32 G triangles.

6. Cut one 3½" by fabric width cream/red print strip; subcut strip into (12) 3½" K squares.

7. Cut three 3⅞" by fabric width strips from each of four blue prints, subcut strips into a total of (116) 3⅞" squares. Cut each square in half on one diagonal to make 232 F triangles.

8. Cut one 3½" by fabric width strip from each of four blue prints; subcut each strip into (12) 3½" K squares.

9. Cut nine 3½" by fabric width brown leaf print strips; subcut strips into (102) 3½" C squares.

10. Cut six 3½" by fabric width royal/navy print strips; subcut strips into (64) 3½" A squares.

11. Cut eight 2¼" by fabric width royal/navy print strips for binding.

12. Cut three 3½" by fabric width cream tonal strips; subcut strips into (36) 3½" B squares.

13. Cut (19) 3⅞" by fabric width cream tonal strips; subcut strips into (190) 3⅞" squares. Cut each square in half on one diagonal to make 380 D triangles.

14. Cut eight 2" by fabric width cream tonal I/J strips.

Project Notes

Pay careful attention to the piecing diagrams for each block and Figure 3 showing the arrangement of the blocks. Separately, the blocks don't really create any design, but when joined, they create a complete overall quilt design, much like the joining of the states to make a much better and more powerful United States of America.

Completing the Blocks

1. Stitch D to E along the diagonal to make a D-E unit, as shown in Figure 1; press seam toward E. Repeat to make 112 D-E units.

Figure 1

2. Stitch D to F along the diagonal to make a D-F unit, again referring to Figure 1; press seam toward F. Repeat to make 228 D-F units.

3. Stitch D to G along the diagonal to make a D-G unit, again referring to Figure 1; press seam toward G. Repeat to make 32 D-G units.

4. Stitch D to H along the diagonal to make a D-H unit, again referring to Figure 1; press seam toward H. Repeat to make eight D-H units.

5. Stitch F to H along the diagonal to make an F-H unit, again referring to Figure 1; press seam toward H. Repeat to make four F-H units.

6. Arrange and join the pieced units in rows with A, B and C squares referring to Figure 2 and the block drawings to complete individual blocks, pressing seams in rows in opposite directions and toward A, B or C when possible.

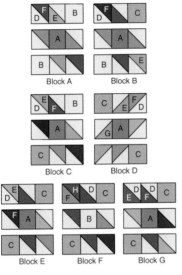

Figure 2

7. Join the rows as pieced to complete the blocks; *do not press seams yet.*

Completing the Quilt

1. Arrange the blocks in rows referring to Figure 3. **Note:** *The * in the figure shows the orientation of the marked corner on each block drawing.*

A	B	C	B	C	B	C	A
C	D	D	G	G	D	D	B
B	D	D	E	E	D	D	C
C	E	E	F	F	E	E	B
B	E	E	F	F	E	E	C
C	D	D	E	E	D	D	B
B	D	D	G	G	D	D	C
A	C	B	C	B	C	B	A

Figure 3

2. Press seams of adjacent blocks in opposite directions, returning each pressed block to the arrangement when pressed.

3. Join blocks in rows as arranged; press seams in adjoining rows in opposite directions.

4. Join the rows to complete the pieced center; press seams in one direction.

5. Join the I/J strips with right sides together on short ends to make one long strip; press seams open. Subcut strip into two 2" x 72½" I strips and two 2" x 75½" J strips.

6. Stitch I strips to opposite long sides and J strips to the top and bottom of the pieced center; press seams toward I and J strips.

7. Trace the heart shape onto the paper side of the fusible web referring to the pattern for number to cut; cut out shapes, leaving a margin around each one.

8. Fuse shapes to the wrong side of the cream/red print fabric; cut out shapes on traced lines. Remove paper backing.

9. Center and fuse a heart shape over the seam between blocks all around quilt edges with pointed end facing I and J strips, and touching seam between strips and blocks as shown in Figure 4 and the Placement Diagram.

Figure 4

10. Cut (16) 4" squares fabric stabilizer; pin a square behind each fused heart shape.

11. Using red thread and a machine satin stitch, stitch all around each heart shape. Remove fabric stabilizer.

12. Select and join remaining C and K squares randomly to make four 25-square strips; press seams in one direction. Set aside extra K squares for another project.

13. Stitch a 25-square strip to opposite sides of the pieced center; press seams toward I strips.

14. Stitch an A square to each end of the remaining pieced strips; press seams toward A. Stitch these strips to the top and bottom of the pieced center to complete the pieced top; press seams toward J strips.

15. Layer, quilt and bind referring to Finishing Your Quilt on page 176. ■

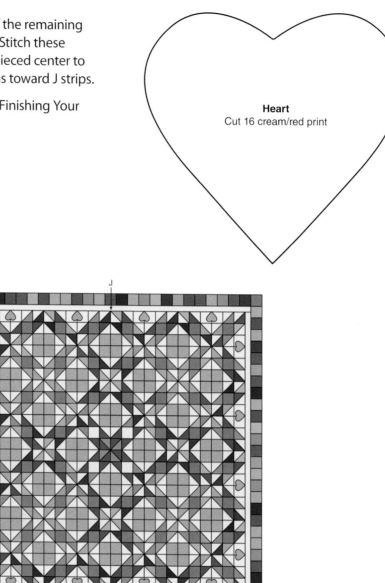

Heart
Cut 16 cream/red print

Mystic Chords of Memory
Placement Diagram 81" x 81"

Stripes & Nine-Patches

The fall colors in this quilt will comfort and warm you all year round.

DESIGN BY SUE HARVEY

PROJECT SPECIFICATIONS

Skill Level: Beginner
Quilt Size: 52¾" x 69½"
Block Size: 13" x 13"
Number of Blocks: 6

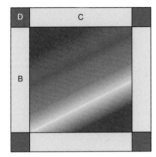

Nine-Patch
13" x 13" Block
Make 6

MATERIALS

- 1 yard gold print
- ⅞ yard multicolor print
- 1¼ yards golden brown tonal
- 2⅛ yards leaf print
- Backing 59" x 76"
- Batting 59" x 76"
- All-purpose thread to match fabrics
- Quilting thread
- Basic sewing tools and supplies

Cutting

1. Cut one 10" by fabric width A strip leaf print.

2. Cut two 6½" x 58" I strips and two 6½" x 53¼" J strips along the length of the leaf print.

3. Cut one 10" x 21" A strip along the length of the leaf print.

4. Cut three 2¼" by fabric width B strips gold print; subcut one strip into two 2¼" x 21" strips.

5. Cut one 10" by fabric width C strip gold print.

6. Cut three 2¼" by fabric width G strips gold print.

7. Cut two 2¼" by 41¼" H strips gold print.

8. Cut two 2¼" by fabric width D strips golden brown tonal.

9. Cut (10) 1¾" by fabric width F strips golden brown tonal.

10. Cut seven 2¼" by fabric width strips golden brown tonal for binding.

11. Cut (14) 1¾" by fabric width E strips multicolor print.

Completing the Nine-Patch Blocks

1. Stitch a fabric-width A strip between two fabric-width B strips with right sides together along length to make a strip set as shown in Figure 1; press seams toward B. Repeat to make another strip set from the 21"-long A and B strips.

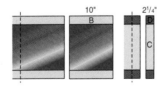

Figure 1

2. Subcut the strip sets into six 10" A-B segments, again referring to Figure 1.

3. Stitch C between two D strips to make a strip set, again referring to Figure 1; press seams toward C.

4. Subcut the strip set into (12) 2¼" C-D segments, again referring to Figure 1.

5. Stitch an A-B segment between two C-D segments to complete one block referring to the block drawing; press seams toward the C-D segments. Repeat to make 6 blocks.

Completing the Nine-Patch Sashing Units

1. Stitch an F strip between two E strips to make a strip set as shown in Figure 2; press seams toward E. Repeat to make 6 strip sets.

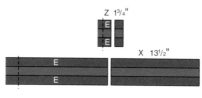

Figure 2

2. Subcut the strip sets into (17) 13½" X units and (12) 1¾" Z segments, again referring to Figure 2.

3. Stitch an E strip between two F strips to make a strip set as shown in Figure 3; press seams toward E. Repeat to make two strip sets.

Figure 3

4. Subcut the strip sets into (24) 1¾" Y segments, again referring to Figure 3.

5. Stitch a Z segment between two Y segments to make a Nine-Patch sashing unit as shown in Figure 4; press seams toward the Z segment. Repeat to make 12 Nine-Patch sashing units.

Figure 4

Completing the Quilt

1. Join two blocks with three X units to make a block row as shown in Figure 5; press seams toward the X units. Repeat to make three block rows.

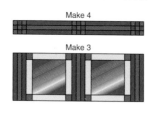

Figure 5

2. Join two X units with three Nine-Patch sashing units to make a sashing row, again referring to Figure 5; press seams toward the X units. Repeat to make four sashing rows.

3. Join the block rows and the sashing rows to complete the pieced center referring to the Placement Diagram for positioning; press seams toward the sashing rows.

4. Join the G strips on short ends to make one long strip; press seams in one direction. Subcut the strip into two 2¼" x 54½" G strips.

5. Stitch the G, H, I and J strips to opposite long sides and then the top and bottom of the pieced center in alphabetical order to complete the top referring to the Placement Diagram for positioning; press seams toward strips.

6. Layer, quilt and bind referring to Finishing Your Quilt on page 176. ▪

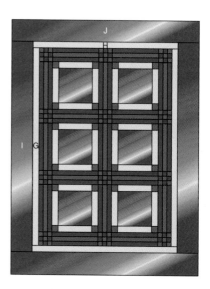

Stripes & Nine-Patches
Placement Diagram 52¾" x 69½"

This & That

The black triangles used in the blocks of this quilt create
a secondary star design when the quilt is complete.

DESIGN BY CONNIE RAND
QUILTED BY LORRAINE SWEET

PROJECT SPECIFICATIONS

Skill Level: Intermediate
Quilt Size: 78" x 90"
Block Size: 12" x 12"
Number of Blocks: 30

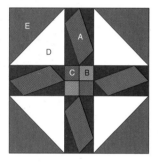

This
12" x 12" Block
Make 15

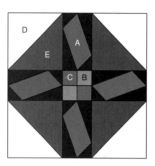

That
12" x 12" Block
Make 15

MATERIALS

- ½ yard each of 5 different black prints
- ½ yard each of 5 different white prints
- ¾ yard purple tonal
- 2⅜ yards black solid
- 3¼ yards blue tonal
- Backing 84" x 96"
- Batting 84" x 96"
- Neutral-color all-purpose thread
- Quilting thread
- Basic sewing tools and supplies

Cutting

1. Cut three 1¾" by fabric width C strips blue tonal.

2. Cut nine 5¼" by fabric width strips blue tonal;
subcut strips into (120) 3" x 5¼" A rectangles.

3. Cut eight 6½" by fabric width strips blue tonal.
Join strips on short ends to make one long strip;
press seams open. Subcut strip into four 6½" x 78½"
J border strips.

4. Cut three 1¾" by fabric width B strips purple tonal.

5. Cut seven 2" by fabric width strips purple tonal.
Join strips on short ends to make one long strip; press
seams open. Subcut strip into two 2" x 72½" F strips
and two 2" x 63½" G strips.

6. Cut two 5⅝" by fabric width strips from each of
the black (E) and white (D) prints. **_Note:_** _Before cutting
strips, select one each black and white print; place fabrics
right sides together and press. Repeat with remaining
black and white fabrics. This saves time matching
triangles for sewing._ Subcut strips into (60) 5⅝" squares
total each color; cut each square in half on one
diagonal to make 120 each D and E triangles.

7. Cut seven 2" by fabric width strips black solid. Join
strips on short ends to make one long strip; press
seams open. Subcut strip into two 2" x 75½" H strips
and two 2" x 66½" I strips.

8. Cut seven 2¼" by fabric width strips black solid;
subcut strips into (120) 2¼" squares. Cut each square in
half on one diagonal to make 120 each pieces 2 and 3
for paper piecing.

9. Cut six 4¾" by fabric width strips black solid; subcut
strips into (120) 2" x 4¾" rectangles. Cut each rectangle
in half to make 120 each pieces 4 and 5 for paper
piecing as shown in Figure 1.

Figure 1

10. Cut nine 2¼" by fabric width strips black solid
for binding.

Completing the This Blocks

1. Sew a B strip to a C strip with right sides together along length to make a B-C strip set; press seam toward B. Repeat to make three B-C strip sets.

2. Subcut the B-C strip sets into (60) 1¾" B-C segments as shown in Figure 2.

Figure 2

3. Join two B-C segments to make a B-C unit as shown in Figure 3; press seam in one direction. Repeat to make 30 B-C units. Set aside 15 units for That blocks.

Figure 3   **Figure 4**

4. Sew D to E to make a D-E unit as shown in Figure 4; press seam toward E. Repeat to make 120 D-E units. Set aside 60 units for That blocks.

5. Pin an A piece right side up on the unmarked side of the Paper-piecing Pattern A. **Note:** *Piece A will cover the entire pattern.*

6. Pin a piece 2 right sides together with A, pinning in place along the marked line between sections 1 and 2 with ¼" extending into section 2 as shown in Figure 5; fold over before stitching to check that it will cover section 2. Adjust as necessary and stitch on the marked side along the line between sections 1 and 2.

Figure 5

7. Turn stitched unit to the fabric side; trim blue and black seam allowance to ⅛"–¼" as shown in Figure 6. Press piece 2 to the right side as shown in Figure 7.

Figure 6   **Figure 7**

8. Repeat steps 6 and 7 with pieces 3, 4 and 5 to complete an A unit referring to Figure 8. Repeat to make 120 A units.

Figure 8

9. Trim fabric edges even with paper pattern referring to Figure 9; set aside 60 A units for That blocks.

Figure 9

10. To complete one This block, sew a B-C unit between two A units to make the center row as shown in Figure 10; press seams toward the B-C unit.

Figure 10

11. Sew an A unit between two D-E units as shown in Figure 11 to make the top row; repeat to make the bottom row. Press seams toward the D-E units.

Figure 11

12. Sew the center row between the top and bottom rows to complete one This block referring to the block drawing; press seams toward the center row.

13. Repeat steps 10–12 to make 15 blocks.

Completing the That Blocks

1. To complete one That block, sew an A unit to each side of a B-C unit to make the center row, again referring to Figure 10; press seams toward the A unit.

2. Sew a D-E unit to opposite sides of an A unit to make the top row as shown in Figure 12; press seams toward the A unit. Repeat to make the bottom row.

Figure 12

3. Sew the center row between the top and bottom rows to complete one That block referring to the block drawing; press seams away from the center row.

4. Repeat steps 1–3 to make 15 blocks.

Completing the Quilt

1. Join three This blocks with two That blocks to make an X row referring to Figure 13; press seams toward This blocks. Repeat to make three X rows.

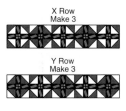

X Row
Make 3

Y Row
Make 3

Figure 13

2. Join three That blocks with two This blocks to make a Y row, again referring to Figure 13; press seams toward This blocks. Repeat to make three Y rows.

3. Arrange and join X and Y rows referring to the Placement Diagram; press seams in one direction.

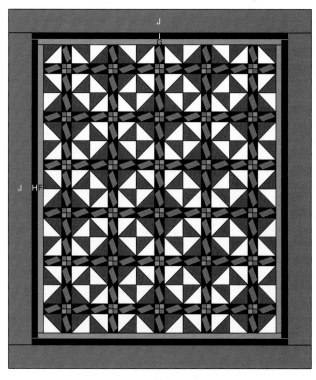

This & That
Placement Diagram 78" x 90"

4. Sew an F strip to opposite long sides and G strips to the top and bottom of the pieced center; press seams toward F and G strips.

5. Sew an H strip to opposite long sides and I strips to the top and bottom of the pieced center; press seams toward H and I strips.

6. Sew a J strip to opposite long sides and to the top and bottom of the pieced center to complete the pieced top; press seams toward J strips.

7. Layer, quilt and bind referring to Finishing Your Quilt on page 176. ■

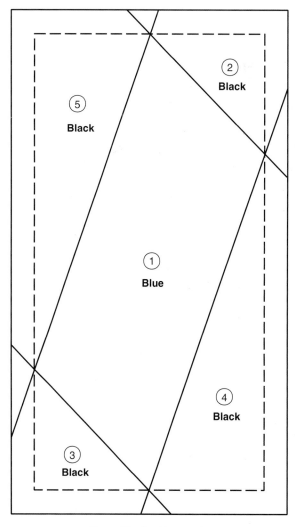

Paper-Piecing Pattern A
Make 120 copies

Flying in Formation

Use toile combined with florals in larger squares to highlight a diagonal path across your quilt top.

DESIGN BY SANDRA L. HATCH
QUILTED BY DIANNE HODGKINS

PROJECT SPECIFICATIONS

Skill Level: Beginner
Quilt Size: 80" x 92"
Block Size: 12" x 12"
Number of Blocks: 30

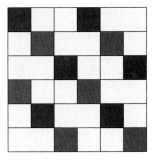

Formation
12" x 12" Block
Make 15

Four-Patch
12" x 12" Block
Make 15

MATERIALS

- ½ yard green tonal
- ⅝ yard red/gold stripe
- 1⅛ yards cream/red toile
- 1⅛ yards red floral
- 1⅓ yards red tonal
- 1¾ yards cream tonal
- 2⅛ yards green large floral
- Backing 86" x 98"
- Batting 86" x 98"
- All-purpose thread to match fabrics
- Hand- or machine-quilting thread
- Basic sewing tools and supplies

Cutting

1. Cut six 6½" by fabric width A strips cream/red toile.

2. Cut three 6½" by fabric width strips each green large floral (B) and red floral (C).

3. Cut six 2½" by fabric width strips each red floral (D) and green tonal (F).

4. Cut (12) 2½" by fabric width E strips cream tonal.

5. Cut six 4½" by fabric width strips cream tonal; subcut strips into (90) 2½" x 4½" G rectangles.

6. Cut (14) 1½" by fabric width strips red tonal. Join strips on short ends to make one long strip; press seams open. Subcut strip into two strips each as follows: 1½" x 72½" H, 1½" x 62½" I, 1½" x 78½" L and 1½" x 68½" M.

7. Cut seven 2½" by fabric width strips red/gold stripe. Join strips on short ends to make one long strip, matching stripe to make a continuous design; press seams open. Subcut strip into two 2½" x 74½" J and two 2½" x 66½" K strips.

8. Cut eight 6½" by fabric width strips green large floral. Join strips on short ends to make one long strip; press seams open. Subcut strip into four 6½" x 80½" N strips.

9. Cut nine 2¼" by fabric width strips red tonal for binding.

Completing the Four-Patch Blocks

1. Sew an A strip to a B strip with right sides together along length to make an A-B strip set; press seams toward B. Repeat to make three strip sets.

2. Subcut the A-B strip sets into (15) 6½" A-B units as shown in Figure 1.

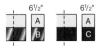

Figure 1

3. Repeat step 1 with A and C strips to complete three A-C strip sets; press seams toward C.

4. Subcut the A-C strip sets into (15) 6½" A-C units, again referring to Figure 1.

5. Join an A-B and an A-C unit as shown in Figure 2 to complete one Four-Patch block; press seam in one direction.

Figure 2

6. Repeat step 5 to make 15 blocks.

Completing the Formation Blocks

1. Sew a D strip to an E strip with right sides together along length to make a D-E strip set; press seam toward D. Repeat for six D-E strip sets.

2. Subcut the D-E strip sets into (90) 2½" D-E units as shown in Figure 3.

Figure 3

3. Repeat steps 1 and 2 with E and F strips to complete 90 E-F units, again referring to Figure 3.

4. Join one D-E unit with one E-F unit to complete a Four-Patch unit as shown in Figure 4; press seam in one direction. Repeat to make 45 units.

Figure 4   **Figure 5**

5. Join one D-E unit with G to make a D-E-G unit as shown in Figure 5; press seam toward D-E. Repeat to make 45 D-E-G units.

6. Repeat step 5 with an E-F unit and G to complete 45 E-F-G units, again referring to Figure 5.

7. Arrange and join the pieced units in rows referring to Figure 6; press seams in adjacent rows in opposite directions.

8. Join the rows, again referring to Figure 6, to complete one Formation block; press seams away from center row.

Figure 6

9. Repeat steps 7 and 8 to make 15 Formation blocks.

Completing the Quilt

1. Join two Four-Patch blocks with three Formation blocks to make an X row referring to Figure 7; press seams toward Four-Patch blocks. Repeat for three X rows.

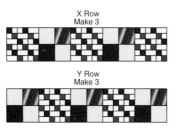

Figure 7

2. Join two Formation blocks with three Four-Patch blocks to make a Y row, again referring to Figure 7; press seams toward Four-Patch blocks. Repeat for three Y rows.

3. Join the X and Y rows referring to the Placement Diagram to complete the pieced center; press seams in one direction.

4. Sew an H strip to opposite sides and I strips to the top and bottom of the pieced center; press seam toward H and I strips.

5. Sew a J strip to opposite sides and K strips to the top and bottom of the pieced center; press seam toward J and K strips.

6. Sew an L strip to opposite sides and M strips to the top and bottom of the pieced center; press seam toward L and M strips.

7. Sew an N strip to opposite sides and to the top and bottom of the pieced center; press seams toward N strips to complete the top.

8. Layer, quilt and bind the quilt referring to Finishing Your Quilt on page 176. ■

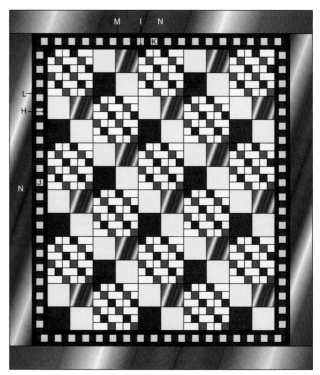

Flying in Formation
Placement Diagram 80" x 92"

Nine-Patch Appliqué Quilt & Bed Runner

Wide borders give a medallion look to the pieced and appliquéd center of this circa 1880–1900 quilt. Appliquéd triangles and squares are an unusual addition to the simple Nine-Patch blocks, plain corner and side triangles. The runner shows how the same block looks in new fabrics.

DESIGN BY SUE HARVEY

Antique Quilt

PROJECT SPECIFICATIONS

Skill Level: Intermediate
Quilt Size: 85½" x 85½"
Block Size: 10½" x 10½"
Number of Blocks: 25

MATERIALS

- 1½ yards yellow print
- 1⅝ yards red solid
- 1⅞ yards green print
- 4¾ yards cream print
- Backing 92" x 92"
- Batting 92" x 92"
- All-purpose thread to match fabrics
- White quilting thread
- Heat-resistant template material
- Spray starch and small brush
- Fabric glue
- Basic sewing tools and supplies

Nine-Patch Appliqué
10½" x 10½" Block
Quilt: Make 25
Runner: Make 2

Cutting

1. Cut four 11" by fabric width yellow print strips; subcut strips into (64) 2¼" x 11" E strips.

2. Cut three 4" by fabric width red solid A strips.

3. Cut six 2" by fabric width red solid strips; subcut strips into (116) 2" C squares.

4. Cut seven 3¼" by fabric width red solid strips; subcut strips into (80) 3¼" squares. Cut each square on both diagonals to make 320 D triangles.

5. Cut (11) 4" by fabric width green print strips. Set aside six strips for B and subcut five strips into (50) 4" M squares.

6. Cut one 3¼" by fabric width green print strip; subcut strips into (12) 3¼" squares. Cut each square on both diagonals to make 48 F triangles.

7. Cut two 2¼" by fabric width green print strips; subcut strips into (24) 2¼" G squares.

8. Cut four 3¾" squares green print; cut each square on both diagonals to make 16 H triangles.

9. Cut (10) 4" by fabric width cream print strips; subcut strips into (100) 4" N squares.

10. Cut two 16⅛" by fabric width cream print strips; subcut strips into two 8⅜" squares and three 16⅛" squares cream print. Cut each 8⅜" square on one diagonal to make four I triangles and each 16⅛" square on both diagonals to make 12 J triangles.

11. Cut two strips each 9" x 70" for K and 9" x 87" for L along length of remaining cream print.

Completing the Appliqué Units

1. Prepare C and D/F appliqué templates using patterns given and heat-resistant template material.

2. Place the C template on the wrong side of a C square as shown in Figure 1. Spray a small amount of spray starch into a small disposable cup. Use the small brush to apply starch to seam-allowance edges extending beyond the template.

Figure 1

3. Press starched edges over the edges of the template using a hot, dry iron. Carefully remove template.

4. Repeat steps 2 and 3 with all C squares.

5. Set aside 32 D triangles. Repeat steps 2 and 3 with the D/F template and the remaining D and F triangles, centering and aligning the long edge of the template with the long edge of the triangles as shown in Figure 2.

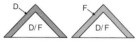

Figure 2

6. Center and align the D/F template on the wrong side of each of the 32 D triangles set aside in step 5. Starch and press only one edge of each triangle, to make 16 each X and XR triangles, as shown in Figure 3.

Figure 3

7. Arrange C, D, F, X and XR pieces on each cream N square and each I and J triangle as shown in Figure 4; pin or use a small amount of fabric glue to hold pieces in place.

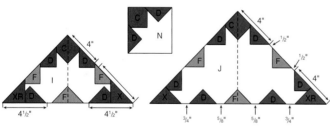

Figure 4

8. Using all-purpose thread to match the appliqué piece in your machine's needle and bobbin, and a blind hemstitch, stitch each piece in place along the turned-under edges.

Completing the Blocks

1. Sew a red A strip between two green B strips to make a strip set; repeat for three strip sets. Press seams toward B.

2. Subcut the strip sets into (25) 4" A segments as shown in Figure 5.

Figure 5

3. To complete one block, sew an M square between two appliquéd N squares as shown in Figure 6; press seams toward M. Repeat to make two M-N units.

Figure 6

4. Sew an A segment between two M-N units to complete one Nine-Patch Appliqué block, again referring to Figure 6; press seams toward the A segment.

5. Repeat steps 3 and 4 to make 25 blocks.

Piecing the Top

1. Join blocks with E strips, and I and J triangles in block rows as shown in Figure 7; press seams toward E strips.

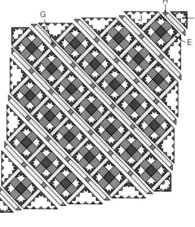

Figure 7

2. Join E strips with G squares and H triangles in sashing rows, again referring to Figure 7; press seams toward E strips.

3. Join the block rows and sashing rows with the two remaining I triangles to complete the pieced center; press seams toward the sashing rows.

4. Referring to the Placement Diagram, sew the K strips to opposite sides and the L strips to the remaining sides of the pieced center; press seams toward strips to complete the top.

Completing the Quilt

1. To make a self-bound quilt, sandwich the batting between the completed top and prepared backing; pin or baste to hold.

2. Hand- or machine-quilt as desired, stopping quilting ¾" from edge of top all around.

3. Remove pins or basting. Trim batting and backing ¾" smaller than top all around.

4. Turn under edge of top ¼" and press. Turn folded edge to back of quilt and pin in place; hand-stitch to back of quilt to finish.

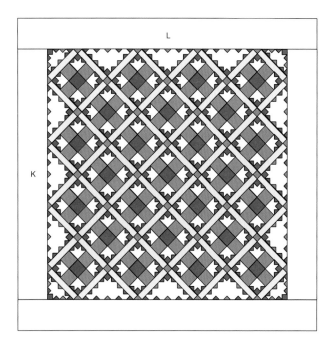

Nine-Patch Appliqué Quilt
Placement Diagram 85½" x 85½"

Runner

PROJECT SPECIFICATIONS

Skill Level: Intermediate
Runner Size: 44¾" x 27⅜"
Block Size: 10½" x 10½"
Number of Blocks: 2

MATERIALS

- ⅓ yard gold print
- ½ yard red print
- ⅝ yard green print
- 1½ yards cream print
- Backing 51" x 34"
- Batting 51" x 34"
- All-purpose thread to match fabrics
- Gold and cream quilting thread
- Heat-resistant template material
- Spray starch and small brush
- Fabric glue
- Basting spray
- Basic sewing tools and supplies

Cutting

1. Cut three 2¼" by fabric width gold print strips; subcut strips into eight 2¼" x 11" E strips.

2. Cut one 2" by fabric width strip red print; subcut strips into (14) 2" C squares.

3. Cut two 3¼" by fabric width red print strips; subcut strips into (14) 3¼" squares. Cut each square on both diagonals to make 56 D triangles.

4. Cut one 4" by fabric width red print strip; subcut strips into two 4" A squares.

5. Cut one 4" by fabric width green print; subcut strip into four 4" B squares and four 4" M squares.

6. From remainder of 4" green print strip, cut two 3¾" squares. Cut squares on both diagonals to make eight H triangles; discard two triangles.

7. Cut one 3¼" by fabric width green print strip; subcut strip into five 3¼" squares. Cut each square on both diagonals to make 20 F triangles; discard two triangles.

8. From remainder of 3¼" green print strip, cut one 2¼" G square.

9. Cut four strips 2¼" by fabric width green print for binding.

10. Cut one 4" by fabric width cream print strip; subcut strip into eight 4" N squares.

11. Cut one 16⅛" by fabric width cream print strip; subcut strip into one 16⅛" square and two 8⅜" squares. Cut each 8⅜" square on one diagonal to make four I triangles. Cut the 16⅛" square on both diagonals to make four J triangles; discard two triangles.

12. Cut four 5½" by fabric width cream print strips; subcut two 5½" x 35¼" for K and two 5½" x 27⅞" for L.

Completing the Top

1. Prepare eight N, four I and two J appliquéd units referring to Completing the Appliqué Units for the antique quilt. **Note:** *Set aside only 12 D triangles in step 5 and prepare only six each X and XR pieces in step 6.*

2. Sew an A square between two B squares to make an A segment; press seams toward B. Repeat to make two A segments.

3. Complete two Nine-Patch Appliqué blocks referring to Completing the Blocks for the antique quilt and then complete the top referring Piecing the Top for the antique quilt, except refer to Figure 8 for stitching block rows and sashing rows.

4. Apply basting spray to one side of the batting; place the prepared backing on the sprayed side, smooth in place. Repeat with the completed top on the remaining side of the batting.

5. Machine-quilt as desired using cream quilting thread in cream print area and gold quilting thread in gold and green print areas. Trim backing and batting even with quilted top.

6. Bind quilt referring to Finishing Your Quilt on page 176. ■

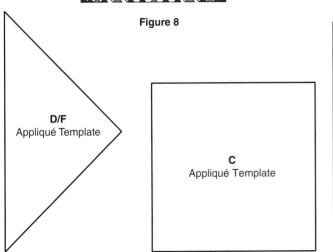

Figure 8

D/F
Appliqué Template

C
Appliqué Template

Nine-Patch Appliqué Runner
Placement Diagram 44¾" x 27⅜"

Clowning Around

Machine-stitched eyes turn the cone-shape pieces around the center of the blocks into clown faces with hats to make this a very special child's quilt.

DESIGN BY KAREN NEARY

PROJECT SPECIFICATIONS

Skill Level: Intermediate
Quilt Size: 53¼" x 72⅜"
Block Sizes: 13½" x 13½" and 4½" x 4½"
Number of Blocks: 6 and 46

Southern Star
13½" x 13½" Block
Make 6

Nine-Patch
4½" x 4½" Block
Make 46

MATERIALS

- ⅛ yard each red, blue, yellow, purple, green, and aqua prints
- ¼ yard peach solid
- ½ yard gold tonal
- 1¼ yards multicolored polka dot
- 2 yards pink tonal
- 2⅛ yards blue tonal
- Backing 60" x 79"
- Batting 60" x 79"
- All-purpose thread to match fabrics
- Black machine-embroidery thread
- Quilting thread
- ¼ yard fabric stabilizer
- Water-erasable marker
- Basic sewing tools and supplies

Cutting

1. Prepare templates A–H using patterns given; cut as directed on each piece transferring all marks with the water-erasable marker.

2. Cut (11) 2" by fabric width N strips blue tonal.

3. Cut three 5" by fabric width blue tonal strips; subcut strips into (24) 5" I squares.

4. Cut five 4" by fabric width J/K strips blue tonal.

5. Cut (13) 2" by fabric width O strips pink tonal.

6. Cut six 4½" by fabric width L/M strips pink tonal.

7. Cut seven 2¼" by fabric width multicolored polka dot strips for binding.

Completing the Southern Star Blocks

1. To complete one block, stitch B to C, matching notched centers, add D and DR as shown in Figure 1. Repeat to make six clown units using a different-color C for each unit. Press D and DR seams away from C; press B seam toward C.

Figure 1

2. Stitch E to the D edge of each clown unit as shown in Figure 2; press seams toward E.

Figure 2

3. Join the pieced units to create an open circle as shown in Figure 3; press seams clockwise toward E.

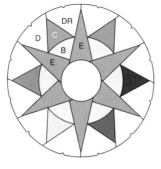

Figure 3

4. Stitch the center of F to the center of D as shown in Figure 4; press seam toward F. Repeat with remaining F pieces to make square corners.

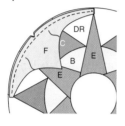

Figure 4

5. Turn under the edge of an A circle ¼" and hand-appliqué in place over the center opening of the pieced unit as shown in Figure 5.

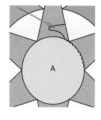

Figure 5

6. Repeat steps 1–5 to make six Southern Star blocks.

7. Cut (36) 1" x 1½" pieces fabric stabilizer; pin one piece behind each B piece.

8. Stitch eyes on B pieces where marked using black machine-embroidery thread and a medium-width zigzag stitch; remove fabric stabilizer.

Completing Nine-Patch Blocks

1. Stitch an O strip between two N strips with right sides together along length to make a strip set as shown in Figure 6; press seams toward N strips. Repeat to make three strip sets.

Figure 6

2. Stitch an N strip between two O strips with right sides together along length to make a strip set again referring to Figure 6; press seams toward N. Repeat to make five strip sets.

3. Cut each strip set into 2" units as shown in Figure 7 to make 46 N-O-N units and 92 O-N-O units.

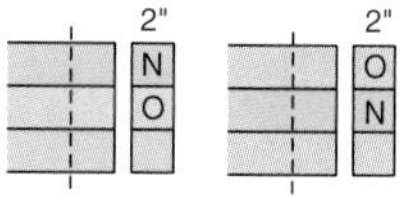

Figure 7

4. Stitch an N-O-N unit between two O-N-O units to complete one Nine-Patch block as shown in Figure 8; repeat to make 46 blocks. Press seams in one direction. Set aside 16 blocks.

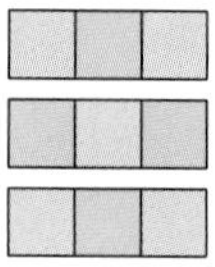

Figure 8

5. Place the G template on one Nine-Patch block and trim as shown in Figure 9; repeat to make 26 G units.

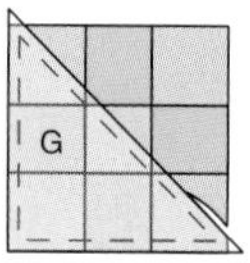

Figure 9

6. Place the H template on one Nine-Patch block as shown in Figure 10; trim to make an H corner unit. Repeat to make four H units.

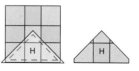

Figure 10

Completing the Quilt Top

1. Join four I squares with five Nine-Patch blocks to make an I section as shown in Figure 11; repeat to make two I sections. Press seams toward I.

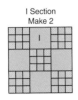

I Section
Make 2

Figure 11

2. Join two I squares with one Nine-Patch block and three G units to make a side section as shown in Figure 12; repeat to make six side sections. Press seams toward I.

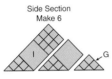

Side Section
Make 6

Figure 12

3. Join one I square, two G units and one H unit to make a corner section as shown in Figure 13; repeat to make four corner sections. Press seams toward I.

Corner Section
Make 4

Figure 13

4. Arrange and join the blocks with the I, side and corner sections in diagonal rows as shown in Figure 14. Press seams in one direction. Join the rows to complete the pieced center.

Figure 14

5. Stitch J/K strips right sides together on short ends; press seams open. Cut two 4" x 38¾" J strips and two 4" x 64⅞" K strips.

6. Referring to the Placement Diagram, sew J strips to the top and bottom, and K strips to opposite sides of the pieced center; press seams toward J and K.

7. Stitch L/M strips right sides together on the short ends; press seams open. Cut two 4½" x 45¾" L strips and two 4½" x 72⅞" M strips.

8. Stitch L strips to the top and bottom, and M strips to opposite sides of the pieced center; press seams toward L and M, again referring to the Placement Diagram.

9. Layer, quilt and bind referring to Finishing Your Quilt on page 176. ■

Clowning Around
Placement Diagram 53¼" x 72⅜"

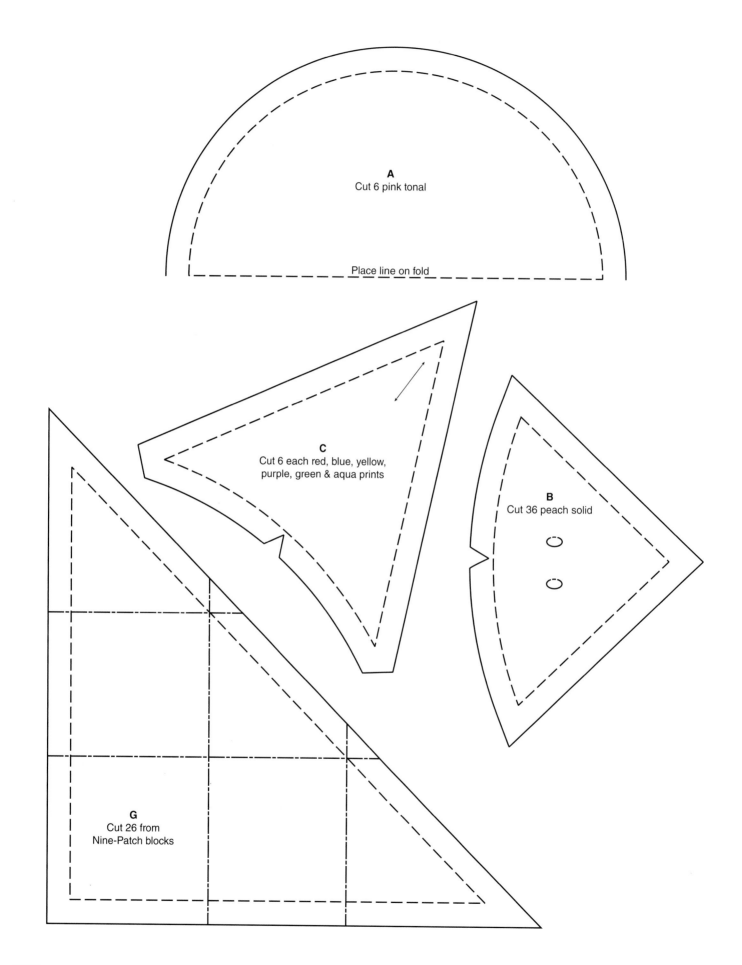

A
Cut 6 pink tonal

Place line on fold

C
Cut 6 each red, blue, yellow,
purple, green & aqua prints

B
Cut 36 peach solid

G
Cut 26 from
Nine-Patch blocks

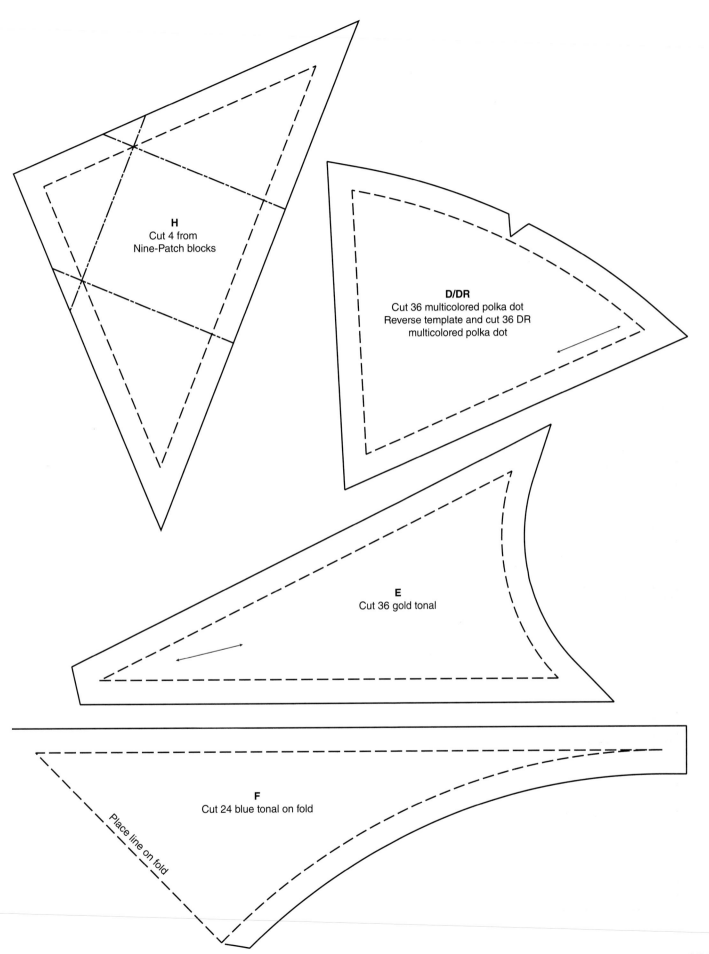

H
Cut 4 from
Nine-Patch blocks

D/DR
Cut 36 multicolored polka dot
Reverse template and cut 36 DR
multicolored polka dot

E
Cut 36 gold tonal

F
Cut 24 blue tonal on fold

Place line on fold

Sweet Nines

Make one of these sweet Nine-Patch projects for yourself or to give as a gift. You will be amazed at all that can be created with this classic block.

In the Meadow

"In the meadow we can build a snowman,"
takes on a whole new meaning in fabric.

DESIGN BY NANCY BORDEAUX OF NANA'S PRETTIES

PROJECT SPECIFICATIONS

Skill Level: Intermediate
Runner Size: 17" x 47"
Block Sizes: 9" x 9" and 3" x 3"
Number of Blocks: 2 and 21

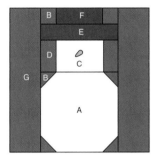

Snowman
9" x 9" Block
Make 2

Blue Nine-Patch
3" x 3" Block
Make 11

Snowball
3" x 3" Block
Make 8

Red Nine-Patch
3" x 3" Block
Make 2

MATERIALS

- Variety red, white and blue fabric strips
- 1 fat quarter black solid
- ⅜ yard navy tonal
- ⅜ yard red tonal
- ⅜ yard white tonal
- ½ yard blue print
- Backing 23" x 53"
- Batting or fusible fleece 23" x 53"
- All-purpose thread to match fabrics
- Quilting thread
- Black embroidery floss
- 2 small carrot buttons
- 2 bird buttons
- 6 (½") black buttons
- Basic sewing tools and supplies

Cutting

1. Cut (20) 1¼"–3" x 21" L/M strips from red, white and blue fabrics.

2. Cut two 1½" x 21" black solid strips; subcut strips into two each 1½" x 3½" F and 1½" x 5½" E strips.

3. Cut four 2¼" by fabric width navy tonal strips for binding.

4. Cut three 1½" by fabric width red tonal I strips.

5. Cut three 1½" by fabric width red tonal strips; subcut strips into two 1½" x 39½" J strips and two 1½" x 11½" K strips.

6. Cut one 5½" by fabric width white tonal strip; subcut strip into two 5½" A squares and two 2½" x 3½" C rectangles.

7. Cut one 3½" by fabric width white tonal strip; subcut strip into eight 3½" H squares.

8. Cut one 2½" by fabric width blue print strip; subcut strip into four 2½" x 9½" G rectangles.

9. Cut five 1½" by fabric width blue print strips. Subcut two strips into four 1½" x 2½" D rectangles and (12) 1½" B squares. Set aside three strips for O.

10. Cut one 1¼" by fabric width blue print strip; subcut strip into (32) 1¼" N squares.

Completing the Snowman Blocks

1. Mark a line from corner to corner on the wrong side of eight B squares.

2. Place a marked B square on each corner of A and stitch on the marked lines as shown in Figure 1; trim seam allowance to ¼" and press B pieces to the right side to complete an A-B unit, again referring to Figure 1. Repeat to make two A-B units.

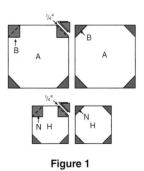

Figure 1

3. Stitch D to each end of C and add E to make a C-D-E unit as shown in Figure 2; press seams toward D and then E. Repeat to make two C-D-E units.

Figure 2

4. Stitch a B square to each end of F; press seams toward B. Repeat to make two B-F units.

5. Join the pieced units as shown in Figure 3 to make a snowman unit; repeat to make two snowman units.

6. Stitch a G strip to opposite long sides of each snowman unit to complete two Snowman blocks; press seams toward G.

Figure 3

Completing the Snowball Blocks

1. Draw a diagonal line on the wrong side of each N square.

2. Place a marked N square on each corner of an H square and stitch referring to Figure 1 in Completing the Snowman Blocks to make one Snowball block. Repeat to make eight blocks.

Completing the Nine-Patch Blocks

1. Stitch an I strip between two O strips along length to make an O-I-O strip set; press seams toward O strips.

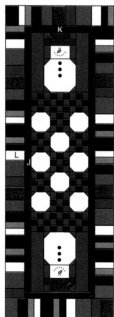

In the Meadow
Placement Diagram 17" x 47"

2. Repeat step 1 with an O strip between two I strips to make an I-O-I strip set; press seams toward O strip.

3. Subcut the O-I-O strip set into (24) 1½" O-I-O units as shown in Figure 4; repeat with the I-O-I strip set to cut (15) 1½" I-O-I units, again referring to Figure 4.

Figure 4   **Figure 5**

4. Stitch an I-O-I unit between two O-I-O units to complete one Blue Nine-Patch block referring to Figure 5; press seams toward the O-I-O units. Repeat to make 11 Blue blocks.

5. Repeat step 4 with one O-I-O unit between two I-O-I units to complete two Red Nine-Patch blocks referring to the block drawing; press seams toward the O-I-O units.

Completing the Runner

1. Stitch a Red Nine-Patch block between two Blue Nine-Patch blocks to make an X row as shown in Figure 6; press seams away from the Blue blocks. Repeat to make two X rows.

X Row
Make 2

Y Row
Make 3

Z Row
Make 2

Figure 6

2. Stitch a Blue Nine-Patch block between two Snowball blocks to make a Y row, again referring to Figure 6; press seams toward Snowball blocks. Repeat to make three Y rows.

3. Stitch a Snowball block between two Blue Nine-Patch blocks to make a Z row, again referring to Figure 6; press seams toward Snowball blocks. Repeat to make two Z rows.

4. Join the X, Y and Z rows to complete the center section referring to the Placement Diagram for positioning of rows; press seams in one direction.

5. Stitch a Snowman block to each end of the center section to complete the pieced center, again referring to the Placement Diagram for positioning; press seams toward Snowman blocks.

6. Stitch a J strip to opposite long sides and K strips to the short ends of the pieced center; press seams toward J and K strips.

7. Join the L/M strips along length to make a strip set at least 21" wide; press seams in one direction.

8. Subcut the L/M strip set into five 3½" L/M units, referring to Figure 7.

9. Join the L/M units on the short ends to make one long strip; press. Subcut the strip into two 3½" x 41½" L strips and two 3½" x 17½" M strips.

10. Stitch the L strips to opposite long sides and M strips to the short ends of the pieced center to complete the pieced top.

3½"

Figure 7

11. Layer, quilt and bind referring to Finishing Your Quilt on page 176.

12. Stitch three black buttons to the center of each snowman A square ¼" from seam and ½" apart.

13. Stitch French knots in a smile shape on each C, ½" from the A/C seam using 2 strands black embroidery floss. Make two eyes 1" above smile using French knots and black embroidery floss.

14. Sew a carrot button between the smile and eyes for nose, and a red bird button by the left-side B-F seam to complete the runner. ∎

Star Bright

Stars shine bright in a blue fabric sky.

DESIGN BY CONNIE CINDLE
QUILTED BY SHERRYL MILLER

PROJECT SPECIFICATIONS

Skill Level: Beginner
Quilt Size: 35" x 35"
Block Size: 8" x 8"
Number of Blocks: 9

Partial Star-in-a-Star
8" x 8" Block
Make 4

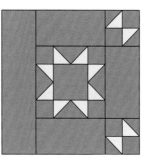

Star
8" x 8" Block
Make 4

Star-in-a-Star
8" x 8" Block
Make 1

MATERIALS

- ⅝ yard yellow dot
- ⅝ yard yellow/blue print
- ⅞ yard navy tonal
- 1¼ yards medium blue tonal
- Backing 41" x 41"
- Batting 41" x 41"
- All-purpose thread to match fabrics
- Quilting thread
- Basic sewing tools and supplies

Cutting

1. Cut five 2½" by fabric width strips medium blue tonal; subcut two of the strips into (52) 1½" x 2½" A rectangles, two strips into (25) 2½" D squares and the remaining strip into four 2½" x 8½" I strips.

2. Cut three 1½" by fabric width strips medium blue tonal; subcut strips into (84) 1½" C squares.

3. Cut four 4½" by fabric width strips medium blue tonal; subcut strips into (50) 2½" x 4½" E rectangles.

4. Cut one 1⅞" by fabric width strip each medium blue tonal (G) and yellow dot (H); subcut each strip into (16) 1⅞" squares.

5. Cut four 1½" by fabric width strips yellow dot; subcut strips into (104) 1½" B squares.

6. Cut three 2½" by fabric width strips navy tonal; subcut strips into (40) 2½" F squares.

7. Cut two 2" x 24½" J strips and two 2" x 27½" K strips navy tonal.

8. Cut three 2½" by fabric width strips yellow dot; subcut strips into (36) 2½" L squares.

9. Cut two 4½" x 19½" M strips and two 4½" x 17½" N strips yellow/blue print.

10. Cut four 2¼" by fabric width strips yellow/blue print for binding.

Piecing the Basic Units

1. Draw a diagonal line from corner to corner on the wrong side of each B, F and H square.

2. Referring to Figure 1, sew B to one end of A along marked line; trim seam to ¼". Press B to the right side. Repeat on the opposite end of A to complete an A-B unit; repeat to make 52 A-B units.

Figure 1

3. Repeat step 2 to make 20 E-F units referring to Figure 2.

Make 20

Make 32

Figure 2

Figure 3

4. Place an H square right sides together with a G square; stitch ¼" on each side of the marked line on H. Cut apart on the marked line as shown in Figure 3 to make two G-H units; press seams toward G. Repeat to make 32 G-H units.

Completing the Star Units

1. To complete one star unit, stitch an A-B unit to opposite sides of D as shown in Figure 4; press seams toward D.

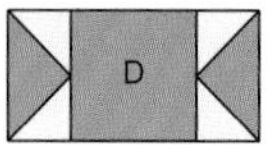

Make 2

Figure 4

Figure 5

2. Stitch C to each end of an A-B unit as shown in Figure 5; press seams toward C. Repeat to make two A-B-C units.

3. Stitch an A-B-C unit to opposite sides of the A-B-D unit to complete a star unit referring to Figure 6; press seams toward the A-B-D unit.

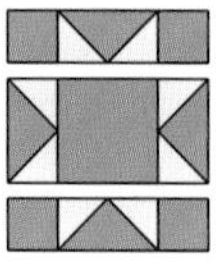

Figure 6

4. Repeat steps 1–3 to make 13 star units.

Completing the Star-in-a-Star Block

1. Stitch an E-F unit to opposite sides of a star unit to make the center row as shown in Figure 7; press seams toward the E-F units.

Make 16

Figure 7

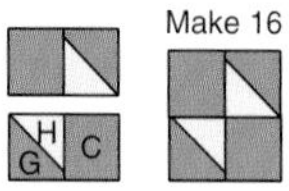

Figure 8

2. Join two G-H units with two C squares to make a corner unit as shown in Figure 8; press seams toward C and in one direction. Repeat to make 16 corner units; set aside 12 units for other blocks.

3. Stitch a corner unit to opposite ends of two E-F units to make two top/bottom rows as shown in Figure 9; press seams toward E-F units.

Make 2

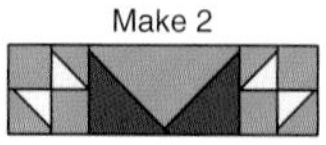

Figure 9

4. Stitch the rows to the top and bottom of the center row as shown in Figure 10 to complete the Star-in-a-Star block; press seams toward the center row.

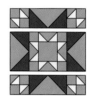

Figure 10

Completing the Partial Star-in-a-Star Blocks

1. To complete one block, stitch an E-F unit to opposite sides of a star unit to make the center row, again referring to Figure 7; press seams toward the E-F units.

2. Stitch D to each end of an E-F unit to make a D row as shown in Figure 11; press seams toward D.

D row

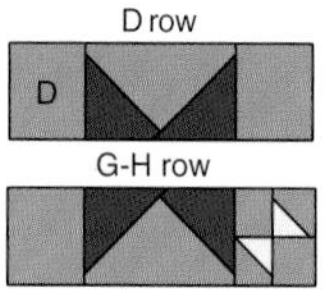

G-H row

Figure 11

3. Stitch D to one end and a corner unit to the opposite end of an E-F unit to make a G-H row as shown in Figure 11; press seams toward the E-F unit.

4. Stitch the D row to one side and the G-H row to the opposite side of the center row to complete one Partial Star-in-a-Star block as shown in Figure 12; press seams toward the center row.

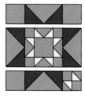

Figure 12

5. Repeat steps 1–4 to make four blocks.

Completing the Star Blocks

1. To complete one block, stitch E to opposite sides of a star unit to make the center row as shown in Figure 13; press seams toward E.

Figure 13   **Figure 14**

2. Stitch a corner unit to each end of E to make a side row as shown in Figure 14; press seams toward E.

3. Stitch the side row to one side and I to the opposite side of the center row as shown in Figure 15 to complete one Star block; press seams toward I and the side row.

Figure 15

4. Repeat steps 1–3 to make four Star blocks.

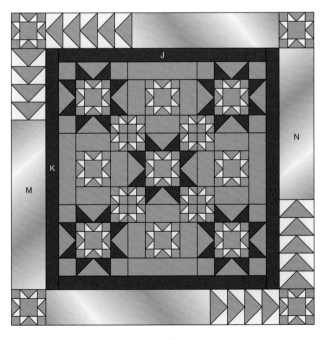

Star Bright
Placement Diagram 35" x 35"

Completing the Quilt

1. Arrange and join the blocks in three rows of three blocks each referring to the Placement Diagram for positioning of blocks; press seams in one direction.

2. Stitch a J strip to the top and bottom, and K strips to opposite sides of the pieced center; press seams toward J and K strips.

3. Mark a diagonal line from corner to corner on the wrong side of each L square.

4. Referring to step 2 for Piecing the Basic Units and Figure 16, complete 18 E-L units.

Figure 16

5. Join four E-L units to make a short E-L strip as shown in Figure 17; press seams in one direction. Repeat to make a second short E-L strip.

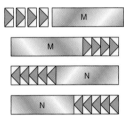

Figure 17

6. Again referring to Figure 17, stitch an M strip to the L side of one short E-L strip; stitch a second M strip to the E end of the second short E-L strip. Press seams toward M.

7. Repeat step 5 with five E-L units each to make two long E-L strips; repeat step 6 with long E-L strips and N strips, again referring to Figure 17.

8. Stitch an E-L-M and E-L-N strip to opposite sides of the pieced center referring to the Placement Diagram for positioning; press seams toward K strips.

9. Stitch a star unit to each end of each remaining strip; press seams toward star units.

10. Stitch a strip to the top and bottom of the pieced center to complete the top; press seams toward J strips.

11. Layer, quilt and bind referring to Finishing Your Quilt on page 176. ■

Optica

A contemporary quilt made with a classic timeless Nine-Patch block—now that's a novel idea!

DESIGN BY TRICIA LYNN MALONEY

PROJECT SPECIFICATIONS

Skill Level: Beginner
Quilt Size: 60" x 60"
Block Size: 12" x 12"
Number of Blocks: 16

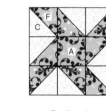

Optica 1
12" x 12" Block
Make 4

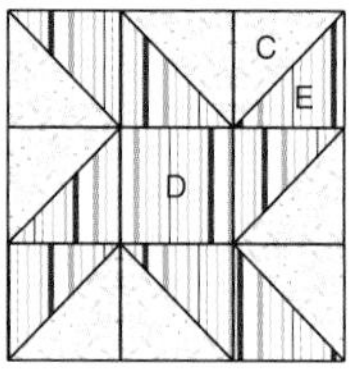

Optica 2
12" x 12" Block
Make 8

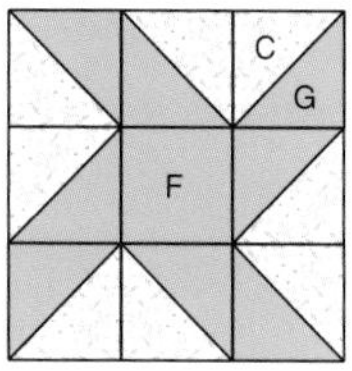

Optica 3
12" x 12" Block
Make 4

MATERIALS

- ⅞ yard coordinating mini-print
- 1⅓ yards coordinating light floral
- 1⅓ yards coordinating stripe
- 1⅜ yards dark floral
- Backing 68" x 68"
- Batting 68" x 68"
- Neutral-color all-purpose thread
- Quilting thread
- Basic sewing tools and supplies

Cutting

1. Cut two 4⅞" by fabric width coordinating mini-print strips; subcut strips into (16) 4⅞" G squares.

2. Cut one 4½" by fabric width coordinating mini-print strip; subcut strips into four 4½" F squares.

3. Cut five 2½" by fabric width coordinating mini-print K strips.

4. Cut eight 4⅞" by fabric width coordinating light floral strips; subcut strips into (64) 4⅞" C squares.

5. Cut one 4½" by fabric width coordinating light floral strips; subcut strips into four 4½" H squares.

6. Cut four 4⅞" by fabric width coordinating stripe strips; subcut strips into (32) 4⅞" E squares.

7. Cut one 4½" by fabric width coordinating stripe strip; subcut strip into eight 4½" D squares.

8. Cut seven 2¼" by fabric width coordinating stripe strips for binding.

9. Cut two 4⅞" by fabric width dark floral strips; subcut strips into (16) 4⅞" B squares.

10. Cut six 4½" by fabric width dark floral strips; subcut one strip into four 4½" A squares. Use five strips for L.

11. Cut two 2½" by fabric width dark floral strips; subcut strips into four 2½" x 4½" I rectangles and four 2½" x 6½" J rectangles.

Completing the Blocks

1. Draw a diagonal on the wrong side of each C square.

2. Layer a C square right sides together with a B square and stitch a ¼" seam on both sides of the diagonal line as shown in Figure 1.

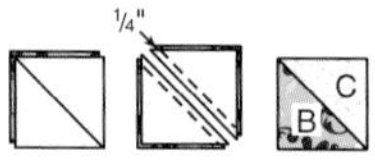

Figure 1

3. Cut on the diagonal line to make two B-C squares, again referring to Figure 1. Press seams toward B.

4. Repeat steps 2 and 3 with all B, C, E and G squares to make 32 B-C squares, 64 C-E squares and 32 C-G squares referring to Figure 2. Label and set aside C-E and C-G squares.

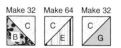

Figure 2

5. Stitch two B-C squares together matching the B sides. Stitch another B-C square matching the C sides as shown in Figure 3 to make top row. Repeat to make bottom row.

Make 2

Figure 3

6. Stitch an A square between two B-C squares, matching B sides to opposite A sides to make center row as shown in Figure 4.

Figure 4

7. Stitch center row between top and bottom rows as shown in Figure 5, matching B edges of the B-C rows to A to make an Optica 1 block.

Figure 5

8. Repeat steps 5–7 to make four Optica 1 blocks.

9. Repeat steps 5–7 with D and C-E squares to make eight Optica 2 blocks referring to the block drawing.

10. Repeat steps 5–7 with F and C-G squares to make four Optica 3 blocks referring to the block drawing.

Completing the Quilt

1. Arrange and join one each Optica 1 and Optica 3 blocks and two Optica 2 blocks to make an X row referring to Figure 6. Repeat to make two X rows.

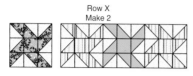

Figure 6

2. Arrange and join one each Optica 1 and Optica 3 blocks and two Optica 2 blocks to make a Y row referring to Figure 7. Repeat to make two Y rows.

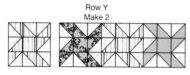

Figure 7

3. Arrange rows as shown in Figure 8. ***Note:*** *Reverse third and fourth rows as indicated.*

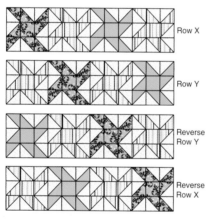

Figure 8

4. Stitch rows together as arranged, matching seams, to complete the pieced center. Press seams in one direction.

5. Stitch an I rectangle to the bottom of H as shown in Figure 9. Press seam toward I.

Figure 9

6. Sew a J rectangle to one side of the H-I unit, again referring to Figure 9. Press seam toward J.

7. Repeat steps 5 and 6 to make four H-I-J corner units.

8. Join the L strips together on short ends to make one long strip; press seams open. Subcut strip into four 4½" x 48½" L border strips.

9. Join the K strips together on short ends to make one long strip; press seams open. Subcut strip into four 2½" x 48½" K border strips.

10. Stitch an L border strip to a K border strip along length to make an L-K border strip; press seam toward L. Repeat to make four L-K border strips.

11. Stitch an L-K border strip to opposite sides of the pieced center referring to Figure 10.

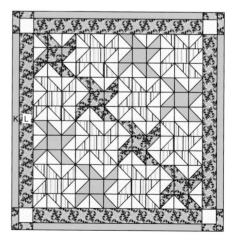

Figure 10

12. Stitch an H-I-J corner unit to both ends of the remaining L-K border strips to make top and bottom borders referring to Figure 11.

Figure 11

13. Stitch the top and bottom borders to the pieced center referring to the Placement Diagram.

14. Layer, quilt and bind referring to Finishing Your Quilt on page 176. ◼

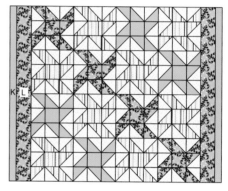

Optica
Placement Diagram 60" x 60"

Nine-Patch Heart Hot Mat

Make a few of these hot mats for all your Valentine friends.

DESIGN BY KATE LAUCOMER

PROJECT SPECIFICATIONS

Skill Level: Beginner
Hot Mat Size: 8½" x 8½"
Block Size: 4½" x 4½"
Number of Blocks: 1

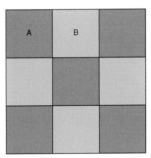

Nine-Patch
4½" x 4½" Block
Make 1

MATERIALS

- Scraps light, medium and dark pink
- 1 fat quarter pink-with-white dot
- Backing 10" x 10"
- Cotton batting 10" x 10"
- Insulated batting 10" x 10"
- All-purpose thread to match fabrics
- Pink machine-embroidery thread
- Template material
- Basic sewing tools and supplies

Cutting

1. Prepare a template for D using pattern given. Cut two D pieces from dark pink scrap.

2. Cut four 2" B squares from light pink scraps.

3. Cut five 2" A squares from medium pink scraps.

4. Cut two 8" C squares from pink-with-white dot; subcut each C square in half on one diagonal to make four C triangles.

5. Cut two 2" x 21" binding strips from pink-with-white dot.

Completing the Nine-Patch Block

1. Referring to the block drawing throughout, stitch a B square between two A squares to make an A-B-A row; press seams toward A. Repeat to make two A-B-A rows.

2. Stitch an A square between two B squares to make a B-A-B row; press seams toward A.

3. Stitch the B-A-B row between two A-B-A rows to complete the Nine-Patch block; press seams in one direction.

Completing the Hot Mat

1. Fold and crease the C triangles on the long side to mark the center.

2. Fold and crease the Nine-Patch block to mark the center.

3. With right sides together, pin the center long-side edge of one C triangle to the center edge of one side of the Nine-Patch block, leaving side edges of C overhanging as shown in Figure 1; stitch. Open C to the right side and press seam allowance toward C.

Figure 1

4. Repeat step 3 with a second C triangle on an adjacent side of the Nine-Patch block as shown in Figure 2. The stitched and pressed unit will look like Figure 3.

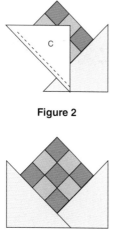

Figure 2

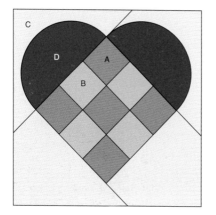

Figure 3

Nine-Patch Heart Hot Mat
Placement Diagram 8½" x 8½"

5. Fold and crease each D piece on the straight edge to mark the center. Turn under the curved edge ¼"; baste in place.

6. Center a basted D piece on each remaining C triangle, matching centers and straight edges; baste to hold in place.

7. Using pink machine-embroidery thread and a machine blanket stitch, stitch around the curved edges of each D piece; remove basting.

8. Referring to steps 3 and 4, and the Placement Diagram, center and stitch the C-D units to each remaining side of the Nine-Patch block, overlapping edges as shown in the Placement Diagram; press seams toward the C-D units.

9. Square up block to 9" x 9", centering the heart shape.

10. Layer as follows: backing, wrong side up; insulated batting, shiny side down; cotton batting; pieced block, right side up. Baste layers to hold. ***Note:*** *Use insulated batting with the shiny side toward the heat source to reflect the heat and better protect your hand.*

11. Quilt and bind referring to Finishing Your Quilt on page 176. ■

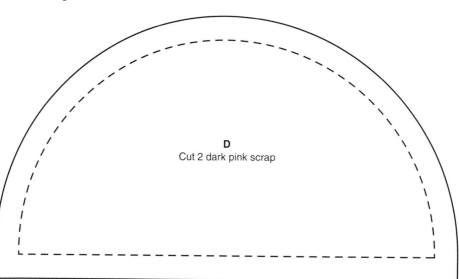

D
Cut 2 dark pink scrap

Basket Table Topper

Simple Nine-Patch blocks combine with appliquéd flower baskets in this small table topper.

DESIGN BY PATRIA SCHINDLER

PROJECT SPECIFICATIONS

Skill Level: Intermediate
Quilt Size: 22½" x 22½"
Block Size: 7½" x 7½"
Number of Blocks: 9

MATERIALS

- 3" x 22" strip gold tonal (D)
- 1 fat quarter each tan plaid, red tonal, green tonal and fruit print
- ⅞ yard muslin
- Backing 28" x 28"
- Batting 28" x 28"
- All-purpose thread to match fabrics
- Quilting thread
- 1 yard 12"-wide fusible web
- ½ yard 22"-wide fabric stabilizer
- (4) ½" black buttons
- Basic sewing tools and supplies

Cutting

1. Cut four 3" x 22" strips muslin for A.

2. Cut five 3" x 22" strips fruit print for B.

3. Cut one strip 3" x 22" red tonal for C.

4. Cut one 8" by fabric width strip muslin; subcut strip into four 8" E squares.

5. Prepare templates for appliqué shapes using patterns given; set aside flower and leaf shapes.

6. Trace four each basket and handle shapes onto the paper side of the fusible web; cut out shapes, leaving a margin around each one. Fuse shapes on the bias of the wrong side of the tan plaid. Cut out shapes on traced lines; remove paper backing.

7. Cut three 2¼" by fabric width strips muslin for binding.

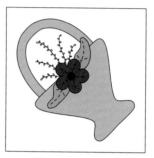

Basket
7½" x 7½" Block
Make 4

Red Nine-Patch
7½" x 7½" Block
Make 4

Gold Nine-Patch
7½" x 7½" Block
Make 1

Completing the Nine-Patch Blocks

1. Stitch an A strip between two B strips to make a strip set; repeat for two strip sets. Press seams toward B; subcut into nine 3" B-A-B segments as shown in Figure 1.

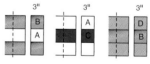

Figure 1

2. Repeat step 1 with one C strip between two A strips to make one strip set; press seams toward C. Subcut strip set into four 3" A-C-A segments, again referring to Figure 1.

3. Cut the D strip and the remaining B strip into two 3" x 11" strips. Stitch one of these B strips between the two D strips; press seams toward D. Subcut strip set into two 3" D-B-D segments, again referring to Figure 1.

4. Join two B-A-B units with one A-C-A unit to complete one Red Nine-Patch block as shown in Figure 2; press seams toward B-A-B units. Repeat to make four Red Nine-Patch blocks.

Figure 2

5. Join two D-B-D units with one B-A-B unit as in step 4 to complete one Gold Nine-Patch block, again referring to Figure 2; press seams toward B-A-B unit.

Completing the Basket Blocks

1. Fold and crease each E square to mark the diagonal centers.

2. To complete one block, center a basket shape on an E square with top of basket ½" above one diagonal centerline as shown in Figure 3. Tuck handle bottom edges under top edge of basket; fuse shapes in place.

Figure 3

3. Pin a square of fabric stabilizer to the wrong side of the fused square.

4. Using thread to match basket fabric, machine zigzag-stitch around edges of handle and basket shapes.

5. Select a fancy machine-embroidery stitch and green thread to stitch a leaf design into the area between the handle and the top of the basket referring to the close-up photo of the block. Remove fabric stabilizer. **Note:** *If your machine does not have this type of design, you may hand-stitch lines for stems and add lazy-daisy stitches for leaves.*

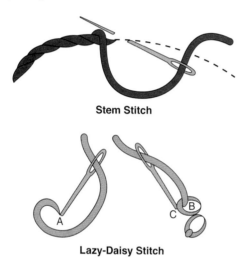

Stem Stitch

Lazy-Daisy Stitch

6. Cut two 6" squares red tonal and layer with right sides together; pin to hold.

7. Trace four flower shapes onto the top layer.

8. With fabrics still layered, stitch around flower shapes on the marked lines.

9. Cut out stitched shapes, leaving 1/16" seam allowance as shown in Figure 4. Cut a slit in one layer of a stitched flower, being careful not to cut through the second layer.

Figure 4

10. Turn flower right side out through the slit; poke out at seams to smooth and press. Repeat to make four flowers.

11. Repeat steps 6–10 with a 10" square of green tonal to make four leaves and four reversed leaves.

12. Pin two leaf shapes on the basket referring to placement lines on basket appliqué motif.

13. Using green thread, zigzag-stitch narrow vein lines on each leaf to secure on basket referring to appliqué motif for placement.

Basket Table Topper
Placement Diagram 22½" x 22½"

14. Pin a flower over the center of the leaves. Using gold thread, zigzag-stitch flower veins on each flower referring to appliqué motif for placement.

15. Hand-stitch a ½" black button in the center of the flower to complete one Basket block.

16. Repeat steps 2–5 and steps 12–16 to make four blocks.

Completing the Top

1. Join one Red Nine-Patch block with two Basket blocks to make a row referring to the Placement Diagram for positioning

of blocks; press seams toward center block. Repeat to make two rows.

2. Join the Gold Nine-Patch block with two Red Nine-Patch blocks to make a row referring to the Placement Diagram for positioning of blocks; press seams toward red blocks.

3. Join the rows to complete the pieced top referring to the Placement Diagram for positioning; press seams in one direction.

4. Layer, quilt and bind referring to Finishing Your Quilt on page 176. ■

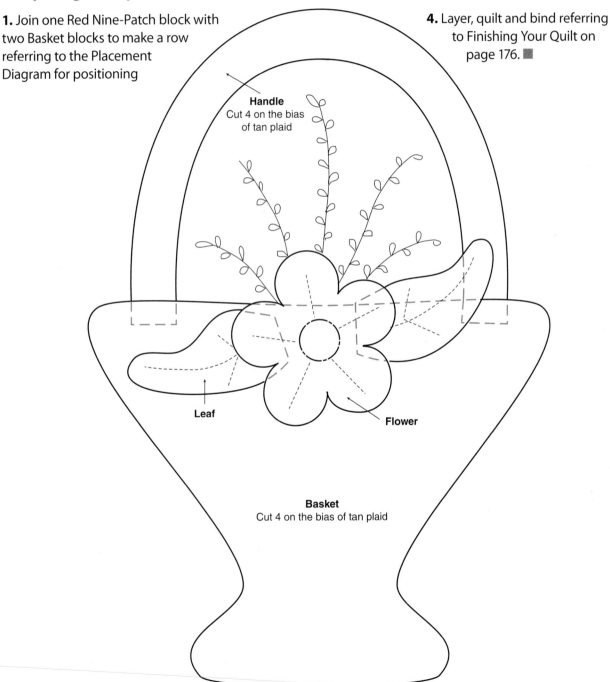

Handle
Cut 4 on the bias of tan plaid

Leaf

Flower

Basket
Cut 4 on the bias of tan plaid

Williamsburg Table Collection

Try a simple technique to make this runner set using reproduction holiday prints.

DESIGN BY MARIA UMHEY

DESIGN BY MARIA UMHEY

PROJECT SPECIFICATIONS

Skill Level: Beginner
Runner Size: 32" x 17"
Candle Mat Size: 17" x 17"
Pot Holder Size: 8" x 8"

Williamsburg Holiday Runner

MATERIALS

- ½ yard cream metallic print
- ½ yard red/green/gold vine print
- ⅝ yard black background holiday print
- Backing 38" x 23"
- Batting 38" x 23"
- All-purpose thread to match fabrics
- Quilting thread
- Basic sewing tools and supplies

Cutting

1. Cut two 6" by fabric width cream metallic print strips; subcut strips into eight 6" A squares and four 5¼" D squares.

2. Cut two 6" by fabric width red/green/gold vine print strips; subcut strips into eight 6" B squares.

3. Cut one 8" by fabric width black background holiday print; subcut strip into an 8" x 23" C rectangle.

4. Cut three 2¼" by fabric width black background holiday print strips for binding.

Completing the Side Units

1. To complete one side unit, layer an A and B square right sides together; cut in half along the diagonal.

2. Sew the resulting A and B triangles together along the diagonal; press seams toward B.

3. Trim each A/B square to 5¼" making sure the seam runs from corner to corner on the square.

4. Layer the two A-B units on a flat surface with wrong sides together and oriented as shown in Figure 1.

Figure 1   **Figure 2**

5. Cut the layered unit into three 1¾" slices as shown in Figure 2.

6. Rearrange the slices and stitch together to make A-B unit and reverse A-B unit as shown in Figure 3; press seams in one direction.

Figure 3   **Figure 4**

7. Join the A-B and reverse A-B units on the 5¼" sides to complete one side unit as shown in Figure 4; press seam in one direction.

8. Repeat steps 1–7 with all A and B squares to make eight side units.

Completing the Runner

1. Join three side units to make a side strip as shown in Figure 5; press seams in one direction. Repeat to make two side strips.

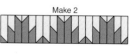

Figure 5

2. Sew a side strip to opposite sides of C referring to the Placement Diagram for positioning of side strips; press seams toward C.

3. Sew a D square to opposite ends of each remaining side unit to make an end strip; press seams toward D squares.

4. Sew an end strip to opposite short ends of C to complete the runner top; press seams toward C.

5. Layer, quilt and bind referring to Finishing Your Quilt on page 176.

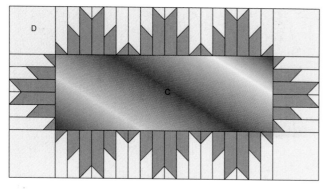

Williamsburg Holiday Runner
Placement Diagram 32" x 17"

Williamsburg Candle Mat

MATERIALS

- 1 fat quarter each black/red/green print, cream/gold print and cream/gold mini print
- ⅓ yard black background holiday print
- Batting 23" x 23"
- Backing 23" x 23"
- All-purpose thread to match fabrics
- Quilting thread
- Basic sewing tools and supplies

Cutting

1. Cut two 6" x 21" black/red/green print strips; subcut into four 6" J squares.

2. Cut two 6" x 21" cream/gold mini print strips; subcut into four 6" I squares.

3. Cut two 5¼" x 21" cream/gold print strips; subcut into four 5¼" E squares.

4. Cut one 8" by fabric width black background holiday print strip; subcut into one 8" F square. Cut

three 2¼" x 34" strips from the remainder of the strip for binding.

Completing the Candle Mat

1. Complete four side units using I and J pieces, and referring to steps 1–7 of Completing the Side Units for Williamsburg Holiday Runner.

2. Sew an I-J side unit to opposite sides of F referring to the Placement Diagram; press seams toward F.

3. Sew an E square to each end of each remaining I-J side unit to make two end strips; press seams toward E squares.

4. Sew an end strip to the remaining sides of F to complete the Williamsburg Candle Mat top; press seams toward F.

5. Layer, quilt and bind using the three binding strips of black background holiday print, referring to Finishing Your Quilt on page 176.

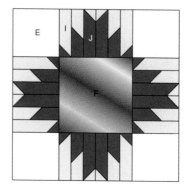

Williamsburg Candle Mat
Placement Diagram 17" x 17"

Holiday Candle Mat

MATERIALS

- 1 fat quarter cream/red/green mini print
- ⅓ yard light background holiday print
- ½ yard cream/gold mini print
- All-purpose thread to match fabrics
- Quilting thread
- Basic sewing tools and supplies

Cutting

1. Cut two 6" x 21" cream/red/green mini print strips; subcut four 6" K squares.

2. Cut one 8" by fabric width light background holiday print strip; subcut one 8" H square. Cut three 2¼" x 34" strips from remainder of strip for binding.

3. Cut two 6" by fabric width cream/gold mini print strips; subcut four 6" I squares and four 5¼" G squares.

Completing the Candle Mat

1. Complete four side units using I and K pieces, and referring to steps 1–7 of Completing the SIde Units for Williamsburg Holiday Runner.

2. Repeat steps 2–4 of Completing the Candle Mat for Williamsburg Candle Mat with H, I-K side units and G squares to complete the Holiday Candle Mat top.

3. Layer, quilt and bind using the three binding strips of light background holiday print, referring to Finishing Your Quilt on page 176.

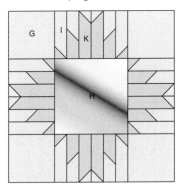

Holiday Candle Mat
Placement Diagram 17" x 17"

Holiday Pot Holder

MATERIALS

- 1 fat eighth black/red/green print
- 1 fat quarter light background holiday print
- Insulating batting 8½" x 8½"
- Cotton batting 8½" x 8½"
- All-purpose thread to match fabrics
- Quilting thread
- Basic sewing tools and supplies

Cutting

1. Cut two 2½" x 21" black/red/green print strips for binding.

2. Cut two 8" L squares from light background holiday print.

Completing the Pot Holder

1. Layer one L square, wrong side up; insulated batting square, cotton batting square and second L square, wrong side down.

2. Baste layers together and quilt as desired

3. Prepare binding referring to Finishing Your Quilt on page 176 using two binding strips of black/red/green print; bind edges of pot holder starting at one corner. When you reach the beginning corner, extend the binding 4½" as shown in Figure 6.

Figure 6

4. Fold the binding extension in ¼" on each raw edge and at the end; stitch to hold.

5. Fold the binding to the back side and hand- or machine-stitch in place around outer edge of pot holder and across extension.

6. Fold the end of the binding extension to the back side to make a hanging loop; stitch to the pot holder as shown in Figure 7. ■

Figure 7

Holiday Pot Holder
Placement Diagram 8" x 8"

In the Woods

Imagine this table runner in shades from nature.

DESIGN BY GUDRUN ERLA

PROJECT SPECIFICATIONS

Skill Level: Intermediate
Quilt Size: 37" x 17¾"
Block Size: 4" x 4"
Number of Blocks: 14

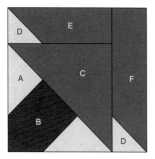

Tree
4" x 4" Block
Make 6

Woods Trail
4" x 4" Block
Make 4

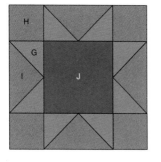

Star
4" x 4" Block
Make 4

MATERIALS

- 1 fat quarter each beige tonal, gold tonal, purple check and green print
- ⅜ yard purple floral
- ⅝ yard burgundy tonal
- Backing 43" x 24"
- Batting 43" x 24"
- Neutral-color all-purpose thread
- Quilting thread
- Basic sewing tools and supplies

Cutting

1. Cut one 2½" x 21" strip beige tonal; subcut strip into six 2½" A squares.

2. Cut one 1½" x 21" strip beige tonal; subcut strip into (12) 1½" D squares.

3. Cut (10) 1" x 21" strips beige tonal; subcut strips into three 1" x 19" R, two 1" x 14½" Q, two 1" x 5½" P and (20) 1" x 4½" O strips.

4. Cut one 4½" x 21" strip green print; subcut strip into six 1½" x 4½" F rectangles. Reduce the width of the strip to 3½" and cut six 1½" x 3½" E rectangles.

5. Cut one 3⅞" x 21" strip green print; subcut strip into three 3⅞" C squares. Reduce the width of the strip to 2½" and cut three 2½" J squares.

6. Cut one 2½" x 21" strip green print; subcut strip into one additional 2½" J square. Reduce the width of the strip to 1½" and set aside for K strip.

7. Cut four 1½" x 21" additional K strips green print.

8. Cut one 3⅞" by fabric width strip burgundy tonal; subcut strip into three 3⅞" B squares. Subcut strip into two 1½" x 14¼" V strips from remainder of strip.

9. Cut two 1½" by fabric width strips burgundy tonal; cut each strip in half to make four 1½" x 21" M strips.

10. Cut two 1½" x 32½" U strips burgundy tonal.

11. Cut three 2¼" by fabric width strips burgundy tonal for binding.

12. Cut four 1½" x 21" strips gold tonal; subcut strips into (16) 1½" x 2½" I rectangles and (16) 1½" H squares.

13. Cut four 1½" x 21" L strips gold tonal.

14. Cut three 1½" x 21" strips purple check; subcut strips into (32) 1½" G squares.

15. Cut one 4⅛" x 21" strip purple check; subcut strip into three 4⅛" S squares and two 2⅜" T squares. Cut each S square on both diagonals to make 12 S triangles and each T square in half on one diagonal to make four T triangles. Set aside two S triangles for another project.

16. Cut one 2½" x 21" strip purple check; subcut strip into four 2½" N squares.

17. Cut two strips each 2½" x 33½" (W) and 2½" x 18¼" (X) purple floral.

Completing the Tree Blocks

1. Mark a diagonal line from corner to corner on the wrong side of each A, C and D square.

2. Referring to Figure 1, place an A square right sides together on opposite corners of B and stitch on the marked lines. Trim seam to ¼" and press A squares to the right sides to complete an A-B unit. Repeat to make three A-B units.

Figure 1

3. Referring to Figure 2, place a C square right sides together with an A-B unit and stitch ¼" on each side of the marked line; cut apart on the marked line and press C to the right side to complete two A-B-C units. Repeat to make six A-B-C units.

Figure 2

4. Referring to Figure 3, place a D square right sides together on one end of E and stitch on the marked line. Trim seam to ¼" and press D to the right side to complete one D-E unit; repeat to make six D-E units.

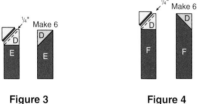

Figure 3   Figure 4

5. Repeat step 4 to make six D-F units referring to Figure 4.

6. To complete one Tree block, stitch a D-E unit to one side and a D-F unit to the adjacent side of an A-B-C unit as shown in Figure 5; press seams toward the D-E and D-F units. Repeat to make six Tree blocks.

Figure 5

Completing the Star Blocks

1. Mark a diagonal line from corner to corner on the wrong side of each G square.

2. Referring to Figure 6, place a G square right sides together on one end of I and stitch on the marked line. Trim seam to ¼" and press G to the right side.

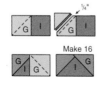

Figure 6

3. Repeat step 2 with G on the opposite end of I to complete a G-I unit, again referring to Figure 6. Repeat to make 16 G-I units.

4. To complete one Star block, sew a G-I unit to opposite sides of J to make the center row as shown in Figure 7; press seams toward J.

Figure 7   Figure 8

5. Sew an H square to opposite ends of two G-I units to make two G-I-H units as shown in Figure 8; press seams toward H.

6. Sew a G-I-H unit to opposite sides of the center row to complete one block referring to the block drawing; press seams away from the center row.

7. Repeat steps 4–6 to make four Star blocks.

Completing the Woods Trail Blocks

1. Stitch K to L to M to K with right sides together along the length to make a K-K strip set as shown in Figure 9; press seams in one direction. Repeat to make two K-K strip sets.

Figure 9

2. Subcut the K-K strip sets into (22) 1½" K-K units, again referring to Figure 9.

3. Stitch K to L to M with right sides together along the length to make a K strip set; press seams in one direction. Subcut the strip set into (10) 1½" K units referring to Figure 10.

Figure 10   Figure 11

4. Stitch L to M with right sides together along the length to make an L-M strip set; press seams toward M. Subcut the strip set into eight 1½" L-M units referring to Figure 11.

5. To complete one Woods Trail block, stitch an L-M unit to opposite sides of N to complete the center row as shown in Figure 12; press seams toward N.

Figure 12

6. Stitch a K-K unit to opposite sides of the center row to complete one Woods Trail block referring to Figure 13; press seams toward the K-K units.

Figure 13

7. Repeat steps 5 and 6 to make four Woods Trail blocks.

Completing the Quilt

1. Sew a K unit to one side of S and a K-K unit to the adjacent side of S as shown in Figure 14; press seams away from S. Repeat to make 10 K-S units.

Make 10

Figure 14

2. Using a rotary cutter and ruler, trim the excess squares even with the long edge of S to complete the side units, again referring to Figure 14.

3. Center and stitch a K-K unit to the long side of T; press seam away from T.

4. Using a rotary cutter and ruler, trim excess squares even with the short edges of T to complete a corner unit as shown in Figure 15; repeat to make four corner units.

Make 4

Figure 15

5. Arrange the blocks in diagonal rows with the O, P, Q and R strips, and the side and corner units referring to Figure 16. Join the blocks with the O strips to make

diagonal rows; press seams toward O. Add side or corner units as needed.

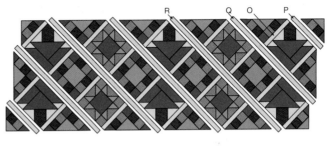

Figure 16

6. Join the rows with the P, Q and R strips; press seams toward the P, Q and R strips. Add remaining corner units to complete the pieced center; press seams toward the P strips.

7. Using a rotary cutter and ruler, trim ends of P, Q and R even with edges of the quilt top as shown in Figure 17.

Figure 17

8. Stitch U strips to opposite long sides and V strips to opposite short ends of the pieced center; press seams toward the U and V strips.

9. Stitch W strips to opposite long sides and X strips to opposite short ends of the pieced center to complete the pieced top; press seams toward the W and X strips.

10. Layer, quilt and bind referring to Finishing Your Quilt on page 176. ■

In the Woods
Placement Diagram 37" x 17³⁄₄"

Stars Around

Showcase a centerpiece on your holiday table with this pretty topper.

DESIGN BY JULIE WEAVER

PROJECT SPECIFICATIONS

Skill Level: Beginner
Quilt Size: 40" x 40"
Block Size: 9" x 9"
Number of Blocks: 12

MATERIALS

- ¼ yard red floral
- ½ yard green tonal
- ½ yard cream tonal
- 1⅛ yards red tonal
- 1¾ yards cream print
- Backing 46" x 46"
- Batting 46" x 46"
- All-purpose thread to match fabrics
- Quilting thread
- Basic sewing tools and supplies

Old Snowflake
9" x 9" Block
Make 12

Cutting

1. Cut two 4¼" by fabric width strips cream print; subcut strips into (12) 4¼" D squares.

2. Cut four 1" by fabric width strips cream print; subcut strips into four 1" x 14½" H strips and four 1" x 17½" L strips.

3. Cut eight 1" by fabric width strips cream print; subcut strips into four 1" x 36½" M strips and four 1" x 39½" O strips.

4. Cut five 2¼" by fabric width strips cream print for binding.

5. Cut seven 3" by fabric width strips cream print; subcut strips into (96) 3" E squares.

6. Cut three 4¼" by fabric width strips red tonal; subcut strips into (24) 4¼" C squares.

7. Cut four 3½" by fabric width strips red tonal; subcut strips into (48) 3½" F squares.

8. Cut two 1½" by fabric width strips red tonal; subcut strips into four 1½" x 15½" J strips.

9. Cut four 1½" by fabric width strips red tonal; subcut strips into four 1½" x 37½" N strips.

10. Cut one 3½" by fabric width strip red floral; subcut strip into (12) 3½" A squares.

11. Cut one 14½" G square cream tonal.

12. Cut two 4¼" by fabric width strips green tonal; subcut strips into (12) 4¼" B squares.

13. Cut one 1½" by fabric width strip green tonal; subcut strip into eight 1½" K squares and (16) 1" I squares.

Completing the Blocks

1. Draw a diagonal line from corner to corner on the wrong side of each B and D square.

2. Referring to Figure 1, layer a B square right sides together with C; stitch ¼" on each side of the marked line.

Figure 1

3. Cut the stitched unit apart on the marked line and press open with seam toward C, again referring to Figure 1 to complete two B-C units. Repeat to make 24 units.

4. Repeat steps 2 and 3 with D and C to complete 24 C-D units referring to Figure 2.

Figure 2

5. Draw a diagonal line across the stitched seam on the wrong side of each C-D unit.

6. Place a B-C unit right sides together with a C-D unit referring to Figure 3, with C pieces matched to B and D; sew ¼" on each side of the marked line, again referring to Figure 3.

Figure 3

7. Cut apart on the marked line, open and press seams in one direction to complete two B-C-D units as shown in Figure 4; repeat to make 48 units.

Figure 4

8. Draw a diagonal line from corner to corner on the wrong side of each E square.

9. With right sides together, place a marked E square on one corner of an F square as shown in Figure 5; stitch on the marked line.

Figure 5

10. Trim seam allowance to ¼"; press E to the right side as shown in Figure 6.

Figure 6

Figure 7

11. Repeat steps 9 and 10 with E on the opposite corner of F to complete an E-F unit as shown in Figure 7. Repeat to make 48 units.

12. To complete one block, sew a B-C-D unit to opposite sides of A to make a center row as shown in Figure 8; press seams toward the B-C-D units.

Figure 8

Figure 9

13. Stitch an E-F unit to opposite sides of a B-C-D unit to make the top row as shown in Figure 9; press seams toward the B-C-D unit. Repeat to make the bottom row.

14. Stitch the top and bottom rows to the center row to complete one Old Snowflake block referring to the block drawing; press seams toward the center row. Repeat to complete 12 blocks.

Completing the Quilt

1. Stitch an H strip to opposite sides of G; press seams toward H strips.

2. Stitch an I square to each end of each remaining H strip; press seams toward H strips.

3. Stitch an H-I strip to the remaining sides of G to make the project center; press seams toward H-I strips.

4. Stitch a J strip to opposite sides of the project center; press seams toward J.

5. Stitch a K square to each end of each remaining J strip; press seams toward J.

6. Stitch a J-K strip to the remaining sides of the project center; press seams toward the J-K strips.

7. Stitch an L strip to opposite sides of the project center; press seams toward L strips.

8. Stitch an I square to each end of each remaining L strip; press seams toward L strips.

9. Stitch an I-L strip to the remaining sides of the project center; press seams toward I-L strips.

10. Join two blocks as shown in Figure 10; press seams in one direction. Repeat to make two two-block units.

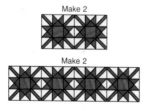

Make 2

Make 2

Figure 10

11. Stitch a two-block unit to opposite sides of the project center; press seams toward the I-L strips.

12. Join four blocks to make a row, again referring to Figure 10; press seams in one direction. Repeat to make two rows.

13. Stitch a row to the remaining sides of the project center; press seams toward the project center.

14. Stitch an M strip to opposite sides of the pieced center; press seams toward the M strips.

15. Stitch an I square to each end of the remaining M strips; press seams toward M strips.

16. Stitch an I-M strip to the remaining sides of the pieced center; press seams toward the I-M strips.

17. Stitch an N strip to opposite sides of the pieced center; press seams toward the N strips.

18. Stitch a K square to each end of the remaining N strips; press seams toward N strips.

19. Stitch a K-N strip to the remaining sides of the pieced center; press seams toward the K-N strips.

20. Stitch an O strip to opposite sides of the pieced center; press seams toward the O strips.

21. Stitch an I square to each end of the remaining O strips; press seams toward O strips.

22. Stitch an I-O strip to the remaining sides of the pieced center to complete the pieced top; press seams toward the I-O strips.

23. Layer, quilt and bind referring to Finishing Your Quilt on page 176. ■

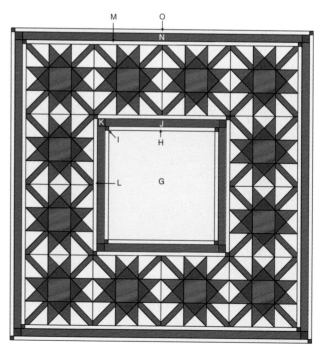

Stars Around
Placement Diagram 40" x 40"

Rose Blue

The cut-off triangles from the block units are perfect for use in a coordinating pillow.

DESIGNS BY TOBY LISCHKO

PROJECT SPECIFICATIONS

Skill Level: Intermediate
Quilt Size: 92" x 102"
Pillow Size: 16" x 16" (without ruffle)
Block Size: 9" x 9" and 3" x 3"
Number of Blocks: 56 and 16

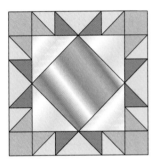

Rose Blue
9" x 9" Block
Make 56

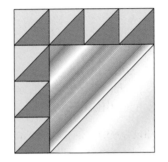

B Bonus
3" x 3" Block
Make 8

MATERIALS

- 1½ yards pink/red tonal
- 2⅛ yards blue/navy tonal
- 2⅛ yards blue/white print
- 2½ yards cream/blue print
- 3⅜ yards blue/white dot
- 4⅓ yards blue floral
- Backing 98" x 108"
- Batting 98" x 108" and 18" x 18"
- Pillow lining 18" x 18"
- Neutral-color all-purpose thread
- Quilting thread
- 16" x 16" pillow form
- Basic sewing tools and supplies

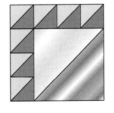

A Bonus
3" x 3" Block
Make 8

Cutting

1. Cut (10) 6½" by fabric width strips blue floral; subcut strips into (56) 6½" A squares.

2. Cut (19) 3½" by fabric width strips cream/blue print; subcut strips into (224) 3½" B squares. Draw a diagonal line from corner to corner on the wrong side of each square.

3. Cut (11) 2" by fabric width strips blue/white dot; subcut strips into (224) 2" C squares.

4. Cut (14) 2⅜" by fabric width strips each blue/white dot (D) and blue/white print (E); subcut strips into (224) 2⅜" squares each fabric. Cut each square in half on one diagonal to make 448 each D and E triangles.

5. Cut (22) 2" by fabric width strips pink/red tonal; subcut strips into (448) 2" F squares. Draw a diagonal line from corner to corner on the wrong side of each square.

6. Cut (11) 3½" by fabric width strips blue/white print; subcut strips into (224) 2" x 3½" G rectangles.

7. Cut five 9½" by fabric width strips blue/navy tonal; subcut strips into (127) 1½" x 9½" H sashing strips.

8. Cut three 1½" by fabric width strips pink/red tonal; subcut strips into (72) 1½" I squares.

9. Cut eight 4½" by fabric width strips blue/white dot. Join strips on short ends to make one long strip; press seams open. Subcut strip into two 4½" x 81½" J strips and two 4½" x 71½" M strips.

10. Cut four 11" P squares blue floral.

11. Cut four 6" Q squares blue/white dot. Draw a diagonal line from corner to corner on the wrong side of each square.

12. Cut eight 2" by fabric width strips cream/blue print. Join strips on short ends to make one long strip; press seams open. Subcut strip into two 2" x 81½" K strips and two 2" x 71½" N strips.

13. Cut eight 5½" by fabric width strips blue floral. Join strips on short ends to make one long strip; press seams open. Subcut strip into two 5½" x 81½" L strips and two 5½" x 71½" O strips.

14. Cut two 2½" by fabric width strips blue floral; subcut strips into two 2½" x 12½" R strips and two 2½" x 16½" S strips.

15. Cut one 11" by fabric width strip blue floral; subcut strip into two 11" x 16½" pillow back rectangles.

16. Cut one 18" by fabric width strip blue/white dot; cut off a 12" right triangle from one end as shown in Figure 1. Cut six 4½" bias strips blue/white dot for pillow ruffle, again referring to Figure 1.

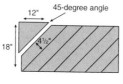

Figure 1

17. Cut (10) 2¼" by fabric width strips blue/navy tonal for binding.

Stitching Bonus Units

To save time and for ease of stitching, you may choose to stitch the bonus units before they are trimmed away from the main unit.

1. Stitch at least ⅜" away from the first stitched seam. *Note: It doesn't really matter if this seam is ½" to create ¼" seams on both cut edges later. The distance between the two seams should not be less than ⅜".*

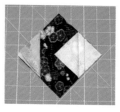

2. Trim between stitched seams using a rotary cutter and ruler.

3. Press the triangles to the right side on both units to create the main unit and the bonus units.

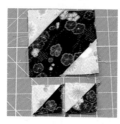

Completing the Rose Blue Blocks

1. Referring to Figure 2, place a B square right sides together on opposite corners of A; stitch on the marked diagonal lines.

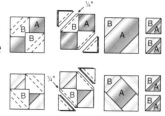

2. Repeat stitching ⅜"–½" from stitched seam, again referring to Figure 2 and the Stitching Bonus Units sidebar. Cut apart between lines and press B open, again referring to Figure 2.

Figure 2

3. Repeat steps 1 and 2 with B on the remaining corners of A to complete an A-B unit and four A-B bonus units, again referring to Figure 2; repeat to make 56 A-B units and 16 A-B bonus units. Set aside bonus units for pillow.

4. Referring to Figure 3, sew F to each end of G as in steps 1 and 2 to complete an F-G unit and two F-G bonus units; repeat for 224 F-G units and 112 F-G bonus units. Set aside the F-G bonus units for the pillow.

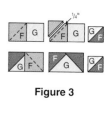

Figure 3

5. Sew E to D along the diagonal to make an E-D unit as shown in Figure 4; press seam toward D. Repeat for 448 E-D units.

Figure 4   **Figure 5**

6. To complete one block, sew an E-D unit to each end of an F-G unit to complete a side unit as shown in Figure 5; press seams toward the F-G unit. Repeat for four side units.

7. Sew a side unit to opposite sides of an A-B unit to complete the center row referring to Figure 6; press seams toward the A-B unit.

Figure 6

8. Sew a C square to each end of each remaining side unit to complete the top row, again referring to Figure 6; press seams toward C. Repeat for the bottom row.

9. Sew the top and bottom rows to the center row referring to the block drawing to complete one Rose

Blue block; press seams toward the center row. Repeat for 56 blocks.

Completing the Quilt

1. Join eight I squares with seven H strips to complete a sashing row referring to the Placement Diagram; press seams toward H. Repeat for nine sashing rows.

2. Join seven Rose Blue blocks with eight H strips to complete a block row again referring to the Placement Diagram; press seams toward H strips. Repeat for eight block rows.

3. Join the sashing rows with the block rows to complete the pieced center, beginning and ending with a sashing row; press seams toward sashing rows.

4. Sew J to K to L with right sides together along length to make a side border strip; press seams away from K. Repeat for two side border strips.

5. Sew a side border strip to opposite long sides of the pieced center; press seams toward side border strips.

6. Place Q right sides together on one corner of P, stitch and trim seam allowance to ¼"; press Q open to complete a corner unit as shown in Figure 7. Repeat for four corner units.

Figure 7

7. Sew M to N to O with right sides together along length to make a top border strip; press seams away from N. Repeat for the bottom border strip.

8. Sew a corner unit to each end of the top and bottom border strips referring to the Placement Diagram for positioning of the corner units; press seams away from the corner units.

9. Sew corner-unit strips to the top and bottom of the pieced center referring to the Placement Diagram for positioning of strips; press seams toward the corner-unit strips to complete the pieced top.

10. Layer, quilt and bind referring to Finishing Your Quilt on page 176.

Completing the Pillow Blocks

1. Trim the F-G bonus units to 1¼" square and the A-B bonus units to 2¾" square referring to the Trimming Bonus Units sidebar at right.

2. To make one A Bonus block, join three F-G units as shown in Figure 8; press seams in one direction.

Figure 8

3. Sew the F-G strip to the B side of an A-B bonus unit as shown in Figure 9; press seam toward A-B bonus unit.

Figure 9

4. Join four F-G units referring to Figure 10; press seams in one direction.

5. Sew the F-G strip to the adjacent side of the pieced A-B-F-G unit to complete an A Bonus block, again referring to Figure 10. Press seam toward the four-piece F-G strip.

Figure 10

6. Repeat steps 2–5 to make eight A Bonus blocks.

Trimming Bonus Units

Sometimes, bonus units are not exactly square after they are stitched, especially if they are very small. They may also be an unusual size, making them hard to use in pieced blocks. They may be trimmed to a smaller and more usable size using the following steps.

1. Press all units with seam allowances toward the darker fabrics.

2. The stitched-and-pressed units for the project in this article are squared to a smaller size. Refer to pattern for the size needed to complete the project.

3. Place a unit on a rotary-cutting mat.

4. Using a rotary ruler with a 45-degree-angle line, place the line even with the seam line on the unit and two adjacent outer edges extending slightly beyond the edges of the ruler; trim.

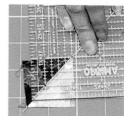

5. Turn the unit, align the 45-degree-angle line with the seam line and align the two trimmed edges with the appropriate-size line on the ruler; trim.

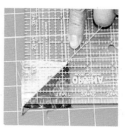

7. Repeat steps 2–5, sewing the F-G strips to the A sides of the A-B bonus units to complete eight B Bonus blocks referring to the block diagram for positioning; press seams as for A Bonus blocks.

Completing the Pillow

1. Join two A Bonus blocks with two B Bonus blocks to make an X row referring to Figure 11; repeat to make two X rows. Press seams in one direction.

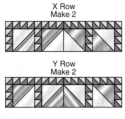

X Row
Make 2

Y Row
Make 2

Figure 11

2. Repeat step 1 to make two Y rows, again referring to Figure 11; press seams in one direction.

3. Join the X and Y rows to complete the pieced pillow center referring to the pillow Placement Diagram for positioning of rows; press seams in one direction.

4. Sew R strips to opposite sides and S strips to the top and bottom of the pieced center; press seams toward R and S strips.

5. Sandwich the batting square between the pieced pillow top and the lining square; quilt as desired by hand or machine.

6. When quilting is complete, trim edges even.

7. Join the 4½"-wide bias strips with diagonal seams as shown in Figure 12 to make a long strip; press seams open. Trim strip to 128".

Figure 12

8. Join the two ends of the strip to make a tube; press seam open.

9. Fold the tube along its length with wrong sides together to make a double-layered tube for ruffle; fold tube into quarters and mark.

10. Stitch a double line of machine basting starting ⅛" from raw edge of ruffle tube with first line and stopping ¼" from marked quarter lines as shown in Figure 13. Leave long threads at each end of stitching.

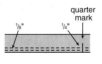

quarter mark

⅛" ¼"

Figure 13

11. Pin the ruffle tube to the sides of the pieced pillow top, matching marked quarter lines to corners.

12. Pull gathering stitches on each side to fit ruffle tube to the pieced pillow top, pinning often to hold in place.

13. Stitch ruffle tube in place, rounding corners slightly when stitching as shown in Figure 14; trim excess at corners.

Figure 14

14. Fold under one 16½" edge of each backing rectangle ¼" and press. Fold under ½" again and press; stitch to hem.

15. Pin the hemmed backing rectangles right sides together with the ruffled, pieced top, overlapping backing rectangles as necessary to fit top as shown in Figure 15; stitch around outside edge using a ¼" seam allowance.

Figure 15

16. Turn pillow right side out through back opening; press to flatten seams.

17. Insert pillow form to finish. ■

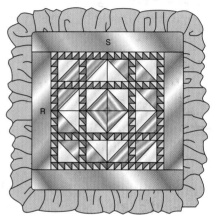

Rose Blue Pillow
Placement Diagram 16" x 16"
(without ruffle)

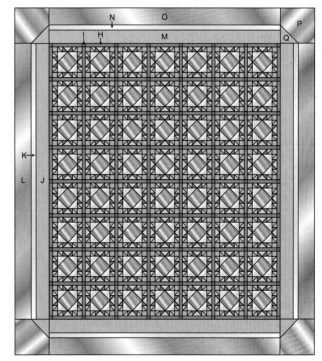

Rose Blue Quilt
Placement Diagram 92" x 102"

Project Gallery

Patriotic Star Log Cabin, 4

Floating Stars, 8

Nine-Patch Squared, 12

Sashed Pinwheels
Bed Runner, 15

Reunion, 18

Got the Blues, 21

Cabin in the Woods, 24

Square Dance, 28

Bloomin' Topper, 32

Blizzard in Blue Bed Quilt, 35

Toile Wreaths, 40

Dewdrops, 43

Romantic Heart, 47

As the Geese Fly!, 50

Nine-Patch Twirl, 53

Beach Buddy, 56

Weathervane Stars, 58

Stars Squared, 63

Royal Cherries, 68

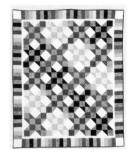
Dots & Prints, 73

An Autumn Evening, 76

Spring Fling, 80

Dragonfly Rings, 84

Swirling Pinwheels, 88

Jitter Buzz, 91

Cartwheels, 98

Four-in-Nine-Patch Zigzag, 102

The Harvester, 105

Wolf Song, 111

Mystic Chords of Memory, 114

Stripes & Nine-Patches, 119

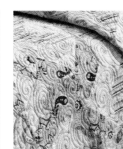
This & That, 122

Flying in Formation, 126

Nine-Patch Appliqué Quilt & Bed Runner, 129

Clowning Around, 134

In the Meadow, 141

Star Bright, 144

Optica, 148

Nine-Patch Heart Hot Mat, 151

Basket Table Topper, 154

Williamsburg Table Collection, 158

In the Woods, 162

Stars Around, 166

Rose Blue, 169

Finishing Your Quilt

1. Press quilt top on both sides; check for proper seam pressing and trim all loose threads.

2. Sandwich batting between the stitched top and the prepared backing piece; pin or baste layers together to hold. Mark quilting design and quilt as desired by hand or machine.

3. When quilting is complete, remove pins or basting. Trim batting and backing fabric edges even with raw edges of quilt top.

4. Join binding strips on short ends with diagonal seams to make one long strip; trim seams to ¼" and press seams open.

5. Fold the binding strip in half with wrong sides together along length; press.

6. Sew binding to quilt edges, matching raw edges, mitering corners and overlapping ends.

7. Fold binding to the back side and stitch in place to finish. ■

Special Thanks

Please join us in thanking the talented designers and quilters below.

Cheryl Adams
Swirling Pinwheels, 88

Chloe Anderson
Dewdrops, 43

Sandy Boobar
Toile Wreaths, 40

Nancy Bordeaux
In the Meadow, 141

Michael L. Burns
Cartwheels, 98
Stars Squared, 63
Wolf Song, 111

Connie Cindle
Star Bright, 144

Michele Crawford
Cabin in the Woods, 24
Dots & Prints, 73

Holly Daniels
Dragonfly Rings, 84

Barbara Douglas
Four-in-Nine-Patch Zigzag, 102

Gudrun Erla
In the Woods, 162

Lucy Fazely
Cartwheels, 98
Stars Squared, 63
Wolf Song, 111

Pat Forke
Patriotic Star Log Cabin, 4

Susan Getman
Royal Cherries, 68

Sue Harvey
Nine-Patch Appliqué Quilt
    & Bed Runner, 129
Stripes & Nine-Patches, 119
Toile Wreaths, 40

Sandra L. Hatch
Flying in Formation, 126
Nine-Patch Squared, 12
Sashed Pinwheels
    Bed Runner, 15

Kim Hazlett
Jitter Buzz, 91

Deborah A. Hobbs
Beach Buddy, 56

Dianne Hodgkins
Flying in Formation, 126

Larisa Key
Romantic Heart, 47

Kate Laucomer
Nine-Patch Heart Hot Mat, 151

Toby Lischko
An Autumn Evening, 76
Rose Blue, 169
Square Dance, 28

Tricia Lynn Maloney
Floating Stars, 8
Optica, 148

Sherryl Miller
Star Bright, 144

Karen Neary
Clowning Around, 134

Connie Rand
This & That, 122

Colleen Reale
Dewdrops, 43

Candy Rogers
Four-in-Nine-Patch Zigzag, 102

Patria Schindler
Basket Table Topper, 154

Karla Schulz
Blizzard in Blue Bed Quilt, 35
Got the Blues, 21
Spring Fling, 80

Norma Storm
Weathervane Stars, 58

Lorraine Sweet
This & That, 122

Rhonda Taylor
As the Geese Fly!, 50

Maria Umhey
Mystic Chords of Memory, 114
Reunion, 18
The Harvester, 105
Williamsburg Table
    Collection, 158

Carolyn S. Vagts
Bloomin' Topper, 32
Nine-Patch Twirl, 53

Julie Weaver
Stars Around, 166